$1700

How to Be a
Small-Cap
INVESTOR

WITHDRAWN

Other Books in the McGraw-Hill Mastering the Market Series

**Essential Guides to Today's Most
Popular Investment Strategies**

How to Be a
Small-Cap
INVESTOR

David B. Newton

McGraw-Hill

New York   San Francisco   Washington, D.C.   Auckland   Bogotá
Caracas   Lisbon   London   Madrid   Mexico City   Milan
Montreal   New Delhi   San Juan   Singapore
Sydney   Tokyo   Toronto

McGraw-Hill

A Division of The McGraw·Hill Companies

1 2 3 4 5 6 7 8 9 0 DOC/DOC 9 0 9 8 7 6 5 4 3 2 1 0 9

ISBN 0-07-047183-5

The sponsoring editor for this book was Roger Marsh, the editing supervisor was Donna Muscatello, and the production supervisor was Elizabeth J. Strange. It was set in Times by Lisa Hernandez of Editorial and Production Services.

Printed and bound by R.R. Donnelley & Sons Company.

This publication is designed to provide accurate and authoritative information in regard to the subject matter covered. It is sold with the understanding that neither the author nor the publisher is engaged in rendering legal, accounting, or other professional service. If legal advice or other expert assistance is required, the services of a competent professional person should be sought.

> *—From a Declaration of Principles jointly adopted by a Committee of the American Bar Association and a Committee of Publishers.*

McGraw-Hill books are available at special quantity discounts to use as premiums and sales promotions, or for use in corporate training programs. For more information, please write to the Director of Special Sales, McGraw-Hill, 11 West 19th Street, New York, NY 10011. Or contact your local bookstore.

 This book is printed on recycled, acid-free paper containing a minimum of 50% recycled de-inked fiber.

CONTENTS

Part Three: Putting It All Together

FOREWORD

David Newton asked that I review his book on the chance that I might provide some opening insights derived from my 35-plus years of varied investment management experience. One must be careful to be precise when dealing with professors, or you won't get a good grade. So I want to share several insights about small-cap investing. First let me say, this book will definitely add to your knowledge about investing in small-cap stocks, but readers will have to develop their own skills and style through practice, because their experiences in the future will no doubt differ somewhat from some of the ideas written here.

Every year investment professionals are confronted by new data, new knowledge, new opinions, and a new environment within which to operate. The only constant is that tomorrow it will all again be different because *change is the investor's only certainty.* Be warned that just about the time you think you know everything, you will be confronted with events that prove you do not. I recall comments from a book written in a previous stock market "go-go era" that anyone over the age of thirty could not compete successfully with the younger investors, because the elders knew too much and were therefore too cautious to capitalize on the dynamic "zoomers" in the market. That idea was soon reversed when the market took its next serious dive.

So I offer the dictum that *the more things change, the more they stay the same.* For example, the under-thirties crowd has again reigned in the 1990s, as mutual fund and other portfolio managers raced for performance with limitless streams of cash. Momentum investing overtook such arcane ideas as security valuation. Small-cap and foreign investing became the thing to do. Some of us old guys have been too reticent to add new money to today's bull market because valuations, as pictured on long-term charts, appear high beyond reason.

I have also been unwilling to turn over client money to a Turkish broker sipping ouzo under an umbrella on the streets of Istanbul.

The purpose of this book is to help investors deal with the uncertainties, change, and paradoxes sure to be encountered in small-cap investing. To assist the author and the readers in this task, I want to find words that impart something in the way of useful tools for the future practitioners of small-cap investing.

This may not be as easy as it seems. A simple surefire formula is often what readers want. But, that very idea brings forth the loud and clear knowledge that "experience" teaches: *there are no such formulas.*

Small-cap investors need to understand what really constitutes investing. You may know what the salesperson or chief financial officer said, but do you *really understand* the business? the risks? the deal? If experience has taught me anything, it is that the securities business is one huge marketing machine designed to transfer money from your pockets, or your clients' pockets, to those of the salesmen and their senior partners. Words are the tools of the salesman. You must learn to know and understand who is selling you what! Incidentally, "salesperson" by other names are known as institutional reps, securities analysts, CEOs, brokers, RIAs, consultants, brothers-in-law, and, yes, even cab drivers, barbers, and shoe-shiners.

The kind of twist on words that I refer to can be illustrated by two of my favorite adages. You will hear someone say, "Joe has invested in thirty-day commodity futures." Now come on! Invested? ... in an option that will be worthless after thirty days, 90 percent of the time? Or you will daily hear variations on this theme: "You invested in XYZ stock? Why? My broker recommended it. What does the company do? I don't know. Then, why did you buy it? He said it would go up and we could make a great profit when the earnings come out next week." This book shows readers that small-cap investing is not a thirty-day event, nor is it a matter of trying to time stock purchases to earnings reports.

What needs to be clearly defined and understood about small-cap stocks is whether you are trying to make money by *trading* or by *investing*. David Newton does an excellent job of focusing on the hallmarks of small-cap *investing*. When trading, your only interest is the future change in price. The security involved is but a vehicle to profit from when buying low and selling high. Time horizons are usually hours, days, or a few weeks. A month is a very long time. The "investment story about the business" is merely the grease on the wheels. Investing on the other hand is enhanced by a different mind-set. Investors consider these things to be important: (a) the nature of the business, (b) the financial history, (c) the business plan, (d) the management skills, and just as important, (e) the values and relative values of the firm. Time horizons are long, measured in years and even unto infinity at time of investment. The stock is your vehicle to participate in the success of the emerging company. That is the heart of Newton's approach to small-cap investing.

My many years of experience point out that it is also very useful to understand the differences between:

> *Gambling*, where the chance of getting your money back or more is a very low probability, and the return is based largely on chance.
>
> *Speculating,* where the odds of getting your money back, plus a higher return, are good, based on certain knowledge and experience.
>
> *Investing*, where the return of your money (and a good return) has a fairly high probability, based on reliable procedures of inquiry and information and on a longer future time horizon.

The student or practitioner of small-cap investing should find these three words and definitions to measure and categorize every proposal to move money from one place to another.

Small-cap investing involves risk. There are even times when it can be demonstrated that cash is a risky investment. Day in and day out the academics, the consultants, and the movers and shakers of the investment world will try to convince you that *risk is volatility*. Period! Don't laugh. Millions of dollars have been spent and earned on defining, calculating, and reporting on portfolio betas. After twenty years of failing to improve portfolio returns, the academics finally agreed that this concept was perhaps not the most useful tool. So now they have switched to volatility defined as the R-squared of portfolio value change as a measurement of risk, and the fees are once again rolling in.

But wait, let's see. If high volatility is high risk then the last thing you ever want to do is invest your money in a small-cap stock that might go up in value a lot, right? Do small-cap stocks unduly place a portfolio at too high a risk? Should you try to reduce your volatility score? You can believe that such portfolios would never have bought stock early on in the life of Microsoft, Cisco, or Dell Computer. When I first quizzed clients and advisors about this issue, there were puzzled looks all around. "I thought it was my job," I said, "to invest money in stocks that would go up, and go up a lot." "Oh, oh," they said, "then that's okay!" They suddenly realized they love up volatility, it's just the down volatility they don't like. You see how important definitions are on a given day?

When it comes to small-cap investing, we have the same definitional problems and more. You cannot believe how many definitions there are for "small-cap." Should the dividing line be set at less than $100 million, $250 million, $500 million, or $750 million in market capitalization? Are two companies with $500 million capitalization, one with sales of $50 million and the other with sales of $500 million, both equally small? And, market cap tends to be very ephemeral. Here today, gone tomorrow. A big jump due to a recommendation by the Motley Fool can turn a micro-cap into a small-cap, or even a large-cap in no time (e.g., *Yahoo!*). But does the company have any tangible business to speak of, measured in sales and earnings? Please, while reading this book be reminded that *market cap giveth and market cap taketh away* by the whims of the auction market, at times having little or nothing to do with a company's operations.

What is one to do? Consider that a more useful and stable measurement of size might be sales. If you examine most small-cap mutual fund portfolios you will be astonished at the number of very, very large companies mixed into the portfolios. Why would that be? Because, that's where the market performance (upside volatility) has come from recently. At the end of the quarter or year, the one thing more important than definitions is *performance.* That is the bottom line taught by experience!

But, wait. It gets more complicated. When the investment industry began to see diminished opportunity to advise on dividing between large-cap and small- cap stocks, they devised categories such as *value* small-cap and *growth* small-cap. It is virtually impossible to find rational definitions for these categories that are actually carried out in portfolios. From stock to stock in a portfolio it all depends on whether you define value in the balance sheet (hardly ever) or in the profit and loss statement (occasionally). Small-cap stocks are most often selected for their "stories," not their existing numbers. The academics may need to find a way to statistically describe the relative merits of good small-cap company stories. And this book offers a start in that direction.

All of the definitions for small-caps take on new meaning when you actually try to invest significant amounts of money in these stocks. True small-caps, however defined, pose a unique set of problems, described and dealt with in this book. These include the lack of research (there is not enough trading to pay for closely watched research); the lack of fair and orderly markets (the dealers make huge profits on the spreads between bid and ask, while most investors cannot trade at that price); and the lack of normal liquidity (you run them up when you are buying, and run them back down again as you sell them). Hence trader skills become as important as investment selection skills.

A fact of life the investor will have to learn to live with is that most small-capitalization companies are not profitable businesses. I concede that in an era of hot high-tech and Internet stocks, any desire to own a company that is profitable and growing is an idea as old as wearing ties to the office and opening car doors for ladies. This is quite important. Most often the market stars involve companies with no earnings. A recent project undertaken to search for new candidates in a database of some 300 to 400 very small companies, selecting those who made a profit last year, then for a series of years, found roughly 60 candidates that could meet that simple requirement. Within six months, despite great "stories" for all, almost half of the 60 had disappointing earnings reports.

Then why all the interest in small-cap investing? First, it is a perfectly logical assumption that a "small" company can grow its value more and faster than is the case for a giant company. Then, back in the 1980s, the academics "proved" and legitimized the idea with some statistical research that returns from small-caps were greater over time than from large-caps. It is rumored that this report was prepared to support four high-powered stock salespersons who needed a new story to sell. Close inspection of the proving charts reveals that such a thesis may or may not be so, depending on the beginning and ending dates chosen. Be wary of making absolute statements of relative historical performance of small-cap stocks. There are a few great winners, but many more great losers.

It is illustrative to compare stocks and investors to cars and drivers. We might consider small-caps to be similar to hot sports cars, mid-caps to good sports sedans, and blue-chips to large cruisers such as Lincolns and Cadillacs. Such comparisons are not unreal. Within such a context, this book has done a good job in giving readers/drivers/would be small-cap investors driving instructions and road maps to guide them down the highways of small-cap investing. But consider that all drivers are not alike in their temperament or skills at driving high-speed, high-performance cars, if you get my meaning. Small-cap highways are littered with wrecks that were perfectly fine autos when they were bought. When presented, small-caps (like sports cars) are all very pretty, some more so than others, some faster than others, some more reliable in completing the desired trip than others. What you end up with depends on the skill and experience of the driver/portfolio manager. This book, like a road map, will help readers gain experience in order to be successful in making small-cap investments.

However, success will only come through the hard-won experience of living through many events and through the development of a personal investment style. As the great Gallagher is famous for insisting, "style" is everything. Perhaps the best comment from Dr. Newton is this: *"Small-cap investing is a systematic discipline that requires prudent selection, patience amid short-term volatility, and an entrepreneurial perspective for long-term appreciation in value."* I would only amend the comment by saying it *"should be"* a systematic discipline, rather than "is." I suspect a study of longer-term outperformers in small-cap investing would reveal that they subscribe to and practice the profession accordingly. Those that came and went in a blaze of glory probably did not. As a final thought, I would commend to the readers' serious musings the idea presented by Dr. Newton's that "small cap investing is itself an entrepreneurial enterprise." This is a valuable observation. Without a positive, can-do attitude, of either an ebullient nature or a quiet studious nature, readers will find their interest in investing in small companies short-lived and not productive.

This is a good book. It does not pretend to have pat answers for a complicated subject. Nor does it offer a surefire formula for success. That said, it offers investors good tools to work with among small-cap stocks. While experienced investors may well say "I know that," I believe they will benefit by treating this book as a refresher course based on a well-designed approach to analysis. Less experienced investors will find this book a solid foundation from which to gain experience in the pursuit of managing a small-cap portfolio.

—Richard C. Taylor,
President, Santa Barbara Asset Management.
Manager, SBAM Small-Cap Model Portfolio

PREFACE

For many individuals, there is nothing quite as exciting as rummaging through a nondescript garage sale, only to come across an item that has tremendous value hidden beneath a generic outward facade. For investors, perhaps nothing is more exciting than purchasing shares of common stock in a relatively small company at a very early stage in the development of the firm, prior to the point where its products or services experience rapid sales growth as part of a newly emerging industry trend. But the processes of mulling over secondhand yard sale items and selecting small company stocks for investment are actually quite different activities. Although they are both about being in the right place at the right time, the former depends on chance, while the latter could be the result of systematic research and hard work. With regard to small-cap investing, the question remains: *Is it possible to locate and systematically invest in a portfolio of public firms that have identifiable characteristics consistent with emerging growth potential as well as smaller market capitalization?*

Every investor would love to uncover the next Microsoft Corporation, Merck Pharmaceuticals, or Gateway Computer early on when the firm is small and relatively unknown. Investors could have purchased shares of Compaq Computer in 1984 for less than five dollars a share had they recognized that "portable" computers would soon become laptops, and ultimately notebooks, with speed and features that rivaled the best of the desktops, mini's, and mainframes. Just a few years earlier, shareholders in Osborne (the original "portable" computer maker) had lost everything when the company closed its doors for good. And yet at the same time that Compaq was poised for extraordinary growth, Kaypro also designed and sold "portable" computers, but through a different strategy and architecture. The rest is history. Compaq is now a household name and the worldwide leader in personal computer sales, while Kaypro, like Osborne, has long since gone out of business. The difference between these three firms was the way each was positioned for the emerging portable-laptop-notebook computer trend, as well as their financial strengths and weaknesses, and other strategic factors.

Smaller companies have several distinctions that separate their common stock from mid-capitalization and large-cap equities in the screening and selection process. There is also a good deal of unique terminology that reflects the financial structure, cash-flow patterns, and product and service introductions of smaller, emerging growth companies that may signal untapped appreciation in value. The objective for investors is to locate the hidden value that many smaller-sized firms provide to those who are actively researching the next widely successful growth industry and product or service innovation.

The Small-Cap System

"How to be a small-cap investor" is actually a multifaceted question. It might infer that there is, in fact, a particular "way" to do this type of investing. The "how" of small-cap investing opens up many issues about an individual's assessments of economic, industry, and company-specific data and analysis. It introduces decision criteria and personal preferences for stock selection into this discussion. The question also raises several issues regarding what exactly constitutes a small-capitalization stock investment. Defining and clarifying this niche within the equities arena has been the subject of much attention among professional portfolio managers and the financial press, as well as academic researchers and individual investors. Finally, the question also introduces a wide range of topics pertaining to the philosophy of managing such an investment.

This book seeks to present a concise overview of contemporary data and information related to this thought-provoking question and seeks to bring clarity and purpose to the investor who is serious about small-cap stock opportunities. These chapters try to cut through years of research studies and evidence concerning small-cap portfolio performance and to discuss an overall investment rationale and strategy geared toward this potentially profitable segment of the capital market. This specific approach to investing does not guarantee consistent double-digit annual returns, but it will clearly identify evidence and processes aimed at emerging-growth industries and the exciting small-cap companies that comprise them.

Topics and Chapter Organization

The first facet of the book addresses the processes and methodologies involved in implementing a small-cap investment strategy. It presents a systematic approach to do this type of investing, which is different in many ways from traditional common stock investment strategies. Readers will learn how to locate a large pool of small-cap stocks from existing public information that can be easily accessed through various reference materials and on-line services. Next, specific procedures and analysis will be introduced to provide a framework for narrowing the pool into a discrete group of small-cap stocks that have indicators consistent with the potential for exceptional future appreciation in price. Also, several approaches to monitoring a small-cap portfolio will be introduced with respect to risk exposure, return expectations, performance evaluations, liquidity preferences, and investment time horizons. The goal is to make small-cap investing practical and rewarding for those with an eye for emerging innovations and untapped product service industry trends.

Chapter 1 introduces the "entrepreneurial" perspective of small-cap investing. Entrepreneurs willingly assume what appear to be significant business risks, but they do so intentionally, with a plan for managing the risk through innovation and marketing ingenuity. The focus of this investment philosophy is aimed at developing a vision for what *might* be possible for the company's stock over time. This requires patience, even when contemporary wisdom does not, as yet, recognize the impending changes that accompany innovation and the advancing of the current knowledge base. Many smaller firms embody the distinguishing profile of entrepreneurial vision, innovation, and emerging product or service markets that are unique to small-capitalization stocks. This supports an underlying rationale and model focused on the potential for extraordinary long-term gains that might come from investing for the long term in firms that display such an entrepreneurial perspective. Chapter 2 then defines these small-cap companies as unique based upon eight characteristics that are typical of fast-growth entrepreneurial ventures. These are set apart from traditional blue-chips (large-cap) and the more mature mid-cap issues.

Chapter 3 presents clear empirical evidence from the NASDAQ, AMEX, and NYSE of how small-cap stocks have historically performed relative to large-caps, mid-caps, and the traditional market. This will help to establish the specific risk-return trade-off within this small-cap market segmentation strategy and how it affects stock selection. This chapter clearly defines companies whose market equity value represents a relatively *small capitalization* when compared to the range of firm values. It also summarizes some of the research questions about whether small-caps really provide a unique investment return.

They may even have different internal managerial agendas for research and development spending, cash-flow distributions, dividend policies, debt financing, and risk tolerance.

Small-cap investing is aimed at joining emerging industries and consumer market trends, in the early stages of development, by purchasing stock in the firms that will have the greatest success with products and services in these potential growth sectors. Chapter 4 discusses fundamental and technical analysis, and the basic levels of research that typically guide the small-cap investment process. Five industry characteristics are presented to help identify innovative product and service offerings that typify strong growth industries. These can be used to rank whether certain industries are well positioned to include rapidly developing product technologies as well as innovative business alliances and services.

Chapter 5 identifies three small-cap firm types and introduces eight screening factors aimed at locating the best small-cap companies in the most promising industries. Small-cap stocks are those firms that are still small enough to be flexible and focused on marketing and innovation success, allowing quicker responses to changes in industry direction and consumer behavior. The screening process is discussed, as are sample firm profiles. Chapter 6 then provides a complete overview of several key financial indicators that characterize firms as small-caps with the strongest upside potential for growth. Special attention is paid to cash flows and a growth index.

Chapter 7 develops a summary of the screening process from the earlier chapters and examines contemporary groupings of small-cap stocks from some of the best small-cap fund managers in the United States, with an emphasis on strong profiles for 1999 and beyond. Also summarized are the basic precepts and concepts that constitute successful small-cap *investor* perspectives. A good deal of research and well-documented tests of empirical models exists that point out several wealth-creation tenets that comprise successful investment philosophies with regard to equity portfolios, risk factors, and time horizons. Equity investors understand that changing information about the financial markets, product and service industries, and a firm's technology and financial position will likely contribute to short-term price volatility. Small-cap investors need to have an eye toward building wealth over the longer-term, and as such, they should be content to weather the interim volatility with expectations for building value over time.

Chapter 8 discusses the benefits and dynamics of diversification in general, and examines the realities of small-cap intragroup diversification strategies and how these can affect portfolio return expectations in the near term and for the long haul. Chapter 9 then presents a clear strategy for balancing individual risk tolerance and performance return expectations using a small-cap asset allocation system. It is unique from traditional asset allocation strategies and the factors that influence the small-cap trading plans. Chapter 10 provides an overview of several samples of small-cap portfolios, their risk composition, diversification and relative volatility exposure issues, asset allocation transitions over time, return expectations, and performance criteria.

The last two chapters focus on the practical implementation of small-cap investment strategies. Chapter 11 addresses some of the most common questions that individuals have about small-cap portfolio construction. It deals with the trade-offs between active and passive management in the small-cap system, as well as investment time horizons, portfolio rebalancing, industry and firm reassessment, and macroeconomic influences in the buy, sell, and hold cycles for emerging entrepreneurial companies. It also covers questions about risk and misconceptions about investing in initial public offers. Chapter 12 offers concluding remarks and areas to watch concerning the overall small-cap portfolio strategy. It provides comments and concerns that will affect the goals and objectives of contemporary small-cap portfolios.

Target Audiences

How to Be a Small-Cap Investor emphasizes a unique "entrepreneurial perspective" to formulate performance objectives for investing in high-growth, emerging businesses. The ultimate goal is to instill in portfolio managers and individual investors a sense of adventure and exploration while screening companies in search of extraordinary opportunities for capital appreciation in small-company common stock. It is anticipated that this work will become a great resource for information about key topics associated with the small-capitalization segment of applied portfolio management. As a "principles of small-cap" book, it seeks to provide a unique balance between institutional-academic rigor, empirical evidence, and practical narrative for the financial professional and the layperson alike. The book is also targeted for applications as a trade book for practitioners in the investments and portfolio management field. Fund managers, wholesale traders, and especially retail brokers will hopefully keep a copy readily available on the bookshelf as a one-stop overview of the small-cap process, concepts, and terminology. Broker-dealers could use the book as part of their in-house training programs for new financial planners and NASD registered representatives to learn how to market this strategy to retail customers and professional clients.

College and university professors can use the book within the traditional investments and portfolio management course pedagogy, as part of a recommended readings list, or as a resource for portfolio construction examples and for student research papers dealing with investment strategy. And, of course, any individual investor who wishes to learn more about his segment of the equity market will hopefully find it easy to read, informative, thought-provoking, and full of practical ideas that can be put to use right away to take advantage of the opportunities in small-cap stocks. The objective is to make it easy to locate, research, and select small-capitalization stocks for an investment portfolio, using a distinctive approach to classify emerging industries, screening prospects for innovative products and services, and performing financial analysis of small-cap profile companies.

This book introduces several new concepts, namely small-cap diversification and small-cap asset allocation, and how to make these tactics work in the practical selection and management process. The book also makes a special effort not to sacrifice any of the classic fundamentals of the institutional-academic rigor, so it should appeal to professionals in the field, offering both theoretical and conceptual principles. The journey into small-cap investing is exciting. Perhaps the next market trendsetter will wind up in your portfolio, not by accident, but because it demonstrated a small-cap profile with signals for significant returns. Remember, the small-cap investor's task is to locate emerging growth, diversify portfolio holdings toward a clearly defined level of risk and *expected* return, maintain the course for the long haul, reallocate stocks over time, and then enjoy the ride. This ride will probably be fast-paced and volatile, but the promising long-term rewards for those who are patient should more than make up for the short-term bumps along the way. Good investing!

David Newton
Santa Barbara, California

ACKNOWLEDGMENTS

I would like to thank everyone who helped make this project run so smoothly over the last year. First, thanks to McGraw-Hill and my editor, Roger Marsh, for endorsing my unique perspective and position on small-cap investing, both early on in the proposal phase of this book, and through to the completion of the manuscript. My many thanks go out to professional small-cap fund managers Ed Larsen, Bernice Behar, Cynthia Liu, Mike Rega, and Eric Cinnamond for their helpful comments and different ideas as they read through preview drafts of various chapters. I also want to thank Josh Yager for sending over several large envelopes with articles, charts, graphs, and all kinds of data dealing with small-cap stock performance. Thanks also to Dick Taylor for his friendship and direct, no-nonsense approach to investing in emerging companies for the long-term; your Foreword definitely set the perfect tone for the thoughts I wanted to communicate in this book. And finally, I want to thank my wife, Kim, my son Jess, and my daughters Katherine, Jennifer, and Christiane for their love, encouragement, and support during the research and writing of this book. All my love to you always.

Getting Started

The Entrepreneurial Perspective on Small-Cap Investing

The mid-to-late 1990s have witnessed tremendous growth in the overall stock market, and a very strong interest in small-capitalization stocks in particular among all levels of investors. In May of 1998, after just two months on the market, the Fidelity Small Cap Fund closed its doors to new investors after raising some $764 million in only two short months.[1] The attraction to small-cap stocks is tied to the fascination investors have with entrepreneurial start-up firms that burst on the scene with revolutionary products and services, and in just a few years redefine an industry and reward the early-stage shareholders with big profits and a stock price that has quadrupled. But the truth is that small-cap investing cannot guarantee positive returns in portfolio. Success will vary based upon several factors, including:

1. The relative size of the portfolio's holdings
2. The effective level of diversification obtained
3. The overall risk profile of the asset mix
4. The expected holding period
5. Competing returns available in the overall stock market
6. Competing returns in "other" asset investments (nonstock)

No matter how knowledgeable the individual manager is about small-capitalization opportunities, and regardless of how informed the decision-making process is regarding evaluation and selection criteria, investing in small-capitalization stocks will always constitute taking a chance on some relatively unknown company that is doing something apparently new and different. Typically, the small-cap company has displayed an initial capability to deliver a highly innovative and/or unique product or a service to a potentially large market. Small-cap investors put their money into these kinds of firms because they (like the target company) possess a very similar entrepreneurial perspective that recognizes opportunity and the financial rewards that can come to those who can clearly articulate a vision of the future, implement that vision through tangible strategies with a talented management team, and aggressively pursue a business dream even when faced with significant obstacles and a lack of general consensus from the broader investment markets and professionals.

The Entrepreneurial Approach

SNAPSHOT

There are numerous writers and researchers in the area of entrepreneurial finance and new-venture development that offer excellent insights about developing a small-cap perspective. Babson College (MA) professor Jeffrey Timmons believes that "there are three primary driving forces behind successful new venture creation—a great founding team, an exceptional opportunity, and the necessary resources."[2] These particular forces must strike a chord with the small-cap investor as well, because building a highly successful small-cap portfolio requires a unique understanding of what constitutes real value in a stock and how equities in this segment of the market are fundamentally differentiated from larger-capitalization issues.

What is it exactly that constitutes an "entrepreneurial perspective"? Small-cap common stock investing requires a distinctively forward-thinking attitude on several fronts. The basic premise of this entrepreneurial approach to investing is that numerous business opportunities appear on the horizon all the time but only a few bold individuals have the initiative, expertise, vision, and determination to pursue the business breakthrough and turn it into a tangible and profitable venture. The small-cap investor should be intent and focused on consistently scanning the business horizon for early growth signals and for the next round of products and services that will have a significant positive impact on consumer, wholesale, and industrial buying trends. An entrepreneurial perspective is willing to provide financial backing to apparently fledgling companies, knowing that these firms have met certain predefined criteria that distinguish their prospects for long-term growth as being "superior," or at least "far above average." The following nine key components uniquely characterize an entrepreneur, and these should also be present in the overall strategy of the small-cap investor's perspective:

1. A penchant for risk-taking rather than an aversion to risk

2. Ability to spot opportunities in early stages of development

3. Highly innovative problem solving

4. Creative ideas that break with traditional approaches

5. A clear vision of what the future will be

6. A keen recognition of the "big picture" when looking at new ideas

7. An unwavering commitment to the venture "cause"

8. Free-markets, competition, and easy new-venture formation

9. A clear focus on fast, significant, and prolonged growth over time

Risk-Taking

Perhaps one of the most fundamental concepts related to small-cap investing is risk-taking. It quickly distinguishes a truly entrepreneurial perspective from one that is content to play it safe and avoid the prospects for failure. The small-cap investor is not content to sit on the sidelines due to risk aversion and earn only a nominal return on portfolio funds. Instead, a portfolio is deliberately and carefully structured to manage the inherent risks of owning equity shares in companies that are not yet *proven* winners in the market. And this ability to accept and manage increased risk is specifically tailored to a portfolio strategy that recognizes that managed risks can be handsomely rewarded by small-cap companies. Small-cap

investors are willing to move off the mainline channel of market information and, through sound research and analysis, uncover potentially profitable companies in unique and somewhat obscure niches. They readily
accept the uncertainty that comes with investing in potentially profitable,
but not yet proven, ideas. The risk-return trade-off does not mean the
small-cap investor is ready to throw portfolio money to the wind, but that
careful homework and due diligence can point to emerging (and possibly
lucrative) product and service markets, and the firms that will provide the
initial leadership during the early stages of takeoff and fast growth.

Figure 1–1 summarizes the fundamental financial relationship between
the level of risk assumed and the corresponding level of *expected* return
necessary to compensate an investor for any given level of risk exposure.
Developed by William Sharpe and John Lintner in the 1960s, the Capital
Asset Pricing Model simply states that for a given level of risk assumed
(measured along the horizontal axis), a rational investor would expect to
receive a directly related *expected* return (the vertical axis) that is com-
mensurate with the risk.[3, 4] The two basic points that would appear to
define all possible combinations of risk and return were (1) the return on

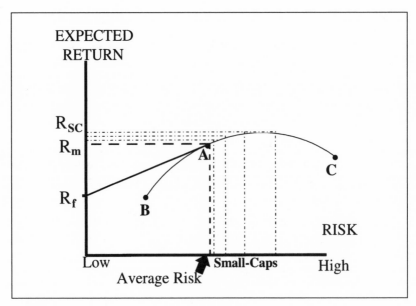

FIGURE 1–1   Capital Asset Pricing Model

an asset that is "free" from risk (R_f) and (2) the return on a fully diversified portfolio of assets that has an average level of "market" risk (R_m and point A). But, they proposed that, in reality, the combinations of risk and return were actually located along a curve that is tangent to point A, so that any initial small increases to low risk probably do not increase an investor's return (point B), and the highest levels of risk would eventually reduce an investor's return (point C). Small-cap investors with an entrepreneurial perspective understand that taking on a relatively higher level of risk is acceptable given the prospects for strong positive returns over the long term (the range of *expected* returns that are targeted by a typical small-cap investor, R_{sc}).

Spotting Opportunity

Small-cap investing is also built on the notion that there are always entrepreneurs inventing and pursuing innovative business ideas, and they create new companies that drive emerging industries. These companies will need to raise capital, and the earliest stock investors will be rewarded for noticing and correctly interpreting these growth signals far in advance of the day they eventually become widely recognized and generally accepted business trends. Consider this excerpt from a recent copy of *American Business Weekly*:

> Somewhere in America today, someone is launching the next huge money-maker. It could be an ingenious way to foster customer loyalty, a retailer turning a generic everyday commodity into a habitual gourmet indulgence, or a brainy kid in a college dorm fast at work on designer DNA, a voice-activated wristwatch, or (who knows?) a molecular food assembler—one for every kitchen.[5]

The process by which a small-cap investor spots an emerging opportunity can be characterized in the following manner. On a regular basis, the various product and service markets send out "weak" signals about new innovations and ideas that are either proposed or "in-the-works." Weak signals start out slow, but they build momentum very rapidly and come to fruition in a relatively short time. These markets also send out "strong" signals which are more predictable and are unfurled at a somewhat slower and steady pace. Figure 1–2 presents both forms of signals that are sent from different locations throughout the many existing product and service

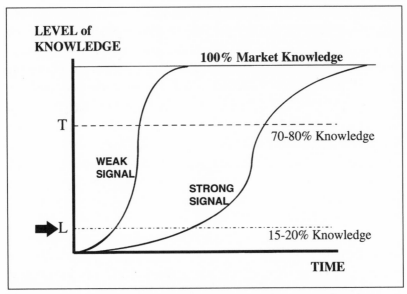

FIGURE 1–2   Weak and Strong Signals of Product and Service Innovations

markets. The level of investor knowledge is measured along the vertical axis, from no knowledge of the emerging signal (trend) on up to full knowledge. The time it takes for the information to be disseminated in the market is measured along the horizontal axis. Weak signals are characterized by a steep and narrow curve, while strong signals are depicted by a gradual and wide curve. The small-cap investor understands that once an emerging product or service reaches a critical threshold of common knowledge (T), the opportunity to profit from the firm's growth may already be passed. An entrepreneurial perspective looks to purchase stocks when knowledge of the event is somewhat low (L), but the potential for long-term profitability and capital appreciation in value is strong.

Innovative Approaches

One of the most important features of any newly emerging business opportunity is the level of innovation that is incorporated into the products and services offered to the market. Innovation can be either continuous or discontinuous in nature. Continuous innovation provides the next logical step in the progression of a product or service development. It adds or updates one or more key features, and it provides a marginal improvement in efficiency, capability, or cost per unit. On the other hand, discontinuous innovation is radical and does not build directly upon the current or recent product and service offerings in the industry. It does not add or update existing features, instead it completely redesigns the entire form and function. It often introduces entirely new products and services that create brand-new markets, which in many instances render the existing products and services obsolete.

Figure 1–3 depicts the four basic types of innovation and market interactions. Type A innovation involves making a gradual, continuous change or improvement to the existing market. Examples can include more fuel-efficient or better-handling automobiles, space-saving appliances, and faster office equipment. Type B innovation means taking that same gradual product or service improvement to a brand-new market. Examples would be the recently created market for coffee. Starbucks made small modifications to what was once a basic (and virtually generic) 50-cent beverage of diners and doughnut shops and turned it into a specialty gourmet drink complete with hundreds of flavor variations at a premium price. The same can be said about Jiffy-Lube. They took a basic oil change from the car dealership or local service station and, with only slight modifications, turned it into a completely new industry based on speed, convenience, and price. The Type

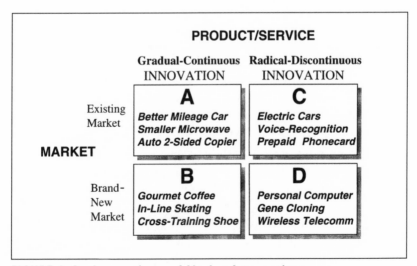

FIGURE 1–3   Innovation and Market Interactions

C form of innovation describes electric-powered automobiles and voice-activated computer software programs. These are radical redesigns that make clean discontinuous breaks from the existing products (gasoline-powered cars and software that must use a traditional keyboard to type in data), but they are targeted toward an already well-established product or service market. The final area, Type D innovation, speaks of radical discontinuous change that introduces entirely new markets. Examples include personal computers, gene cloning, and wireless communications.

The small-cap investor must have an ear tuned to the signals of emerging innovations in the consumer, wholesale, and industrial markets. The portfolio should thrive on stocks that represent forward-thinking companies that introduce innovative ideas with the potential to impact large and growing areas across numerous market segments. This does not always mean that the innovation has to be Type C or Type D. Recent history has clearly demonstrated that tremendous opportunities for small-cap investing can be found among Type B innovations, and even among Type A products and services. The entrepreneurial perspective can also thrive on finding small-cap companies that make products or provide services that are just subcomponents of the innovation championed by one or two pioneering firms. Great profit potential and growth can be found with a small-cap firm that makes the electronic switching device that is used in a major new product introduction.

Creative Thinking

Innovative solutions are often the result of the individual efforts of people who think about problems in unique ways that allow for new approaches to be tried. Failure is viewed as a basic component that helps to press knowledge forward in order to bring about the eventual answers to the questions originally posed. Entrepreneurs are typically very creative in how they view problems and in the approaches they employ to come up with new solutions. Small-cap investing requires a good degree of creativity. Investors must be able to look at potential stock purchases as supporting a proven track record of individual and corporate creativity. The companies invested in are trying new ideas and working on solutions in different and exciting directions that might, one day, very well become industry standards. Putting money behind such creative efforts is what successful small-cap investing is all about.   However, there are risks in backing what appear to be highly differentiated forms of product or service creativity.   Often times some of the most basic products and services used in everyday living were at one time considered dramatically different when they were first created and designed. For example, someone created the 65-degree bend in the middle of the standard computer keyboard and that opened the floodgates for scores of ergonomically engineered office tools, peripherals, and equipment.

Bold Vision

It's one thing to be creative, and another thing to be truly innovative. But what makes creativity and innovation translate into tangible products and high-demand services is entrepreneurial vision. This ability to grasp a clear perspective of the future, viewed from the context of what one truly believes *will* be the case (as opposed to what one *hopes* or *thinks* it might be) is what distinguishes visionary investing from wishful thinking. Small-cap firms often exemplify a view toward the future, bringing the next wave of products and services nearer and closer than they have ever been. A wristwatch color television that can now be purchased for less than $400 is someone's vision finally realized. Investors who believed that there would be a huge market for stand-alone personal computing, were rewarded for their ability to see beyond mainframes. Stockholders who envisioned clear, low-cost, wireless telecommunications reaped huge gains when that concept of the future was made a reality. And today, chemists and mechanical engineers have the vision that trains will be powered by superconductivity and automobiles will be fueled by hydrogen or renewable solar energy. Small-cap investors desire to share in these visions when they are still on the drawing board or being formulated in the lab or tested on the track.

Recognizing the "Big Picture"

Patented gadgets are neat to touch and see, especially when they can do something very astounding or groundbreaking. But how does a "nifty" spectacle in the laboratory become a cost-efficient, highly profitable, and viable product for years to come? And how do specialized chemical, biological, or electronic applications of technology and processes turn into mainstream services that gain quick and widespread acceptance among a clearly targeted market segment? The answer is once again part of the entrepreneurial perspective, namely, having the ability to recognize the "big picture." This involves seeing how an idea can be applied to the lives of everyday consumers and households or become part of several industrial processes. Small-cap investors must be able to see beyond what is merely a fascinating tool or a provocative design. They must recognize the clear link that a company has proposed to take this process or design and make it a tangible product or service for a very large and identifiable target market. That is when investing for the big picture can really generate significant returns. The industrial engineer who formulated an interesting glue variation that did not stick all that well may not have seen the huge need for Post-it® notes, but someone at 3M recognized that there was in fact a worldwide big-picture application for this seemingly trivial product feature. Great ideas are only as good as the extent to which they generate widespread appeal and demand for tangible products and services.

Undaunted Commitment

One of the potential drawbacks to the entrepreneurial perspective of small-cap investing is also one of the greatest necessities required for success in this market segment. It is imperative that small-cap investors develop and maintain a long-term commitment to the venture. Nascent businesses will experience a wide range of adversities during the formative years. It usually takes a good deal of time for a firm to gain a strong competitive position in an industry. The entrepreneurial perspective is one of total commitment to the "cause," namely, the long-term success of the business as it struggles through times of sales volatility, ever-changing cost structures, and fluctuating profitability. Small-cap investors must be patient and remain focused on the long-term goals of the company, even when the near term is fraught with questions and uncertainty.

Free-Market Philosophy

The small-cap investor should also have a keen sense of which markets are truly wide open to new product and service introductions. The investor should understand how such markets are characteristically different from markets that present significant barriers to entry and/or a high degree of government regulation and bureaucracy. There really is not much sense investing in a product that might require six or seven years of testing before it can receive federal approval for the market. Or buying stock in a company that is trying to break into a 25-year-old industry in which three dozen companies are firmly entrenched and that requires more than $50 million in start-up costs just to join in. Small-cap investors should first be looking at emerging industries that have significant potential for a wide range of product and service introductions over the next several years. The best of these markets are typically wide open for new competition and somewhat minimally regulated (or unregulated) to allow for quick entry, reasonable start-up costs, and easy access and transfer of information. Competition will be difficult no matter where investments are made. There is no need to make it even harder by purchasing stocks that come with the added pressures of a slow-moving, crowded, highly regulated, and somewhat noncompetitive environment.

EXTRAORDINARY GROWTH

The small-cap investor typically has a strong appetite for significant and prolonged growth in the portfolio's value over the longer term. Capital appreciation is far more desirable than current dividend income. This expectation is directly related to the overall entrepreneurial perspective of investing. It recognizes that there are really no reliable strategies by which to profit from quick turnarounds in the market. Investing is not viewed as a "timing" issue aimed at getting into stocks just before they have a short-term increase in price, and then selling as they top out. Instead, the rationale underlying small-cap investing is based on joining promising emerging businesses as an equity partner in the early stages of market development, and then staying aboard for the long term to share in the financial rewards as the venture secures a solid competitive position in the industry. Small-cap investors are not interested in earning an 8 percent annual return in low-risk cash flows or even a 15 percent to 20 percent annual growth in value that could double their money in four years. The focus is clearly set on buying shares at around 10 to 15 percent of their future value five or seven years from now. This kind of growth is measured as a factor of 7 or 10 times the original investment.

Income Versus Growth Emphasis

Small-cap investing will many times involve making a fundamental decision between providing the portfolio with quarterly dividends or zero cash flow with an expectation for sizable capital appreciation in stock values over time. Figure 1–4 compares the basic differences between an income emphasis as opposed to a growth, or capital appreciation, emphasis. In the first case, the expectation of periodic cash flow becomes a significant component in the overall risk and valuation position of the firm. Less risky firms like, 1 and 2, are able to distribute net profits to the shareholders in the form of quarterly dividends because they have exhausted all the available options to invest those cash flows internally. More risky firms, like 3, are those that forgo paying dividends and instead reinvest almost all of their profits back into the company's asset base and operations toward the goal of continued growth. Additional evidence suggests that small-cap investors would rather forgo quarterly dividends in exchange for pure capital appreciation in stock values over time, like position 4.

The small-cap investor needs to focus on the prospects for increases in shareholder value as the company expands its product and service lines, manufacturing and support operations, marketing and promotions impact, and corporate identity in the industry among various competitors. In fact, the firm should probably not be paying dividends to shareholders because

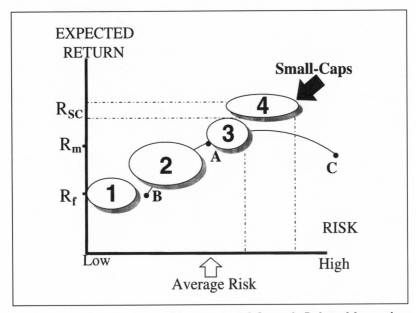

Figure 1–4   Comparison of Income- and Growth-Related Investing

profits are being channeled to numerous investment projects that must be funded in order to remain well positioned in the external market environment. Cash flow is not a component of the small-cap portfolio rationale. Participating in the long-term growth of the emerging business is far and away the primary objective of the small-cap investor.

RESEARCH TIP

The primary objective of the entrepreneurial perspective of small-cap investing is to create a systematic process whereby dozens of promising companies are regularly reviewed and screened through a consistent set of criteria in order to highlight firms that demonstrate extraordinary potential for sustained growth over time. Such a program should not be looking for "hot tips" about stocks that are ready to increase in value quickly due to some short-term announcement or temporary position in a certain market play. Instead, the most successful small-cap investing regimen involves a good deal of fundamental research into company product and service distinctives, financial structure, management capabilities, and partnership value with an eye toward strong positioning in a large and promising market. Hard work will pay off in the long term. Small-cap companies require patience from investors. Research shows very clearly that the strongest performance returns are typically realized by portfolios that maintained stock positions for more than five years and were not subjected to sporadic selling and rebuying in attempts to "time" market movements. The ability to "see" value and recognize the vision for innovative products and services remains the hallmark of the small-cap research process.

Notes

1. Tam, Pui-Wing, 1998. "Is Now a Good Time to Shift Into Small-Cap Stock Funds?" *The Wall Street Journal Interactive Edition*, May 15, www.wsj.com.

2. Timmons, Jeffry A., 1989. *The Entrepreneurial Mind: Winning Strategies for Starting, Renewing, and Harvesting New and Existing Ventures* (Andover, MA: Brick House Publishing Company), p. 8.

3. Sharpe, William F., 1964. "Capital Asset Prices: A Theory of Market Equilibrium Under Conditions of Risk," *Journal of Finance*, No. 19, September, pp. 425–442.

4.   Lintner, John, 1965. "Securities Prices, Risk, and Maximal Gains from Diversification," *Journal of Finance*, No. 20, December, pp. 587–616.

5.   Levinas, Daniel A., 1998. "The Next Billion-Dollar Idea," *American Business Weekly*.

Defining Small-Capitalization Common Stocks

S mall-capitalization common stocks are quite a fascinating component of the U.S. publicly traded markets. A general rule of thumb
states that a small-cap firm has common stock market capitalization
of less than $1 billion. However, some managers prefer the range $500
million to $1 billion, and they refer to firms with capitalization of less than
$500 million as micro-cap stocks. Most investors consider firms with
market capitalization over $5 billion to be large-cap stocks, while others
draw the line at $4 billion or even $3 billion. And at various points between the $1 billion low end and the $5 billion high end are firms generally referred to as mid-caps, although, once again, there are some differences
among fund managers where small-cap ends and mid-cap begins.

There also are numerous instances where it can be quite difficult to
categorize a firm. Take for example the mid-to-late 1990s IPO Internet
stock phenomenon involving firms like Yahoo!, Amazon.com, America
Online, and Netscape. Many of these fast-growth Internet stocks had no-
ticeably small-cap-oriented financial statements, and yet they were considered mid-cap or even large-cap firms by most industry stock value
criteria. In fact, as of July 1998, Amazon.com had an apparently large-cap
market valuation in excess of $5 billion (about the same as the combined
values of Borders Books and Barnes and Noble) and yet had lower revenues than these two firms and only about one-tenth the combined earnings.[1]

For almost three decades now (from the 1970s through the 1990s), investors have heard a good deal of news about the great opportunities for significantly higher profits in the small-cap firms of the NASDAQ market and the Russell 2000 Index versus the large-capitalization firms that comprise the Dow Jones Industrial Average or the Standard and Poor's 500. The most pressing issue is whether there are clear definitions about what exactly makes a company a small-cap investment, and do these firms truly outperform their large-cap and mid-cap counterparts. There are literally several hundred (if not a thousand or more) published articles and doctoral dissertations that have examined the features, trading behavior, price stability, information release, and return performance of these small-cap firms. This chapter will focus on covering all the major topics that help to define a company's stock as being a small-capitalization issue. It will also examine how these concepts affect each other and the overall perception of these firms by different investors. Once the typical small-cap firm is clearly defined, the following chapter will examine the historical track record of investment performances for this category of stocks and draw some interesting comparisons with the mid-cap and large-cap issues.

Segmented Markets

There are many investment experts today who believe that the stock market is actually segmented into two distinct pools of companies. The first pool is composed of large-capitalization stocks that are primarily purchased in large blocks at the wholesale level by institutional investors such as mutual funds, insurance companies, pension funds, trust funds, and investment banks. The second group consists of small-capitalization stocks that are typically bought in smaller lots by small investment clubs and individual investors at the retail level. Most large institutional accounts have prescribed limits on small-cap holdings in their portfolio, so there is a finite level of participation from the big-money funds in this sector of the market. This segmentation implies that institutional portfolios are then the explicit driving force that actually creates and supports efficient markets. It suggests that smaller investors, investing in small-cap stocks, are buying and selling in an inefficient manner that is contrary to the generally accepted market thinking at the top tiers. If this line of market activity reasoning holds, then small-cap stocks could very well be a highly segmented market that operates with distinct differences from those factors and behaviors that influence price movements in the mid-cap and large-cap stocks. (Market capitalization is the total number of shares of common stock outstanding, times the price per share in the market.)

Large-Caps

In the United States, there are less than 400 firms that can boast a market capitalization in excess of the typical $5 billion threshold.[2] Companies such as General Electric, IBM, Merck, Exxon, Proctor and Gamble, and Coca-Cola are known by traders all around the world, and each have a market capitalization in excess of $100 billion, while firms like Ford Motors, GTE, McDonald's, and Dell Computer are relatively smaller, but still have market values of more than $40 billion each.[3] Information about large-cap firms is plentiful and readily available to virtually all levels of traders in the various markets. The top-tier institutional investors such as insurance companies, mutual funds, banks, and pension funds, tend to focus their research and analysis efforts on large-cap stocks, and this in turn creates a disproportionate amount of financial and industry information on this market segment. These stocks often pay steady quarterly dividends and have much more reliable earnings than their small-cap counterparts.

Mid-Caps

Many companies that were not too long ago defined as emerging start-ups, have grown in size and become very popular with mainstream investment professionals. But they are still not quite in the same league with the $40 billion and $100-plus billion large-cap firms. These mid-cap companies may resemble small-caps with slightly higher price volatility and earnings variance compared to the large-caps, but they tend to have greater (and much more reliable) information available about products, market competition, the industry, financials, and senior management. Firms such as Steelcase, Host Marriott, Office Depot, Circuit City Stores, United Airlines, and Yahoo! each have market capitalization of between $3.9 billion and $4.9 billion. Some mid-caps start to pay steady dividends to shareholders, but earnings estimates can still be somewhat less reliable compared to the large-caps, because of rapid product and industry changes as well as increased foreign and domestic competition.

Micro-Caps

At the lowest end of the market-capitalization range reside the smallest of the publicly traded stocks, often referred to as the micro-caps. Just as there are differences in where analysts and portfolio managers draw the lines between large-cap, mid-cap, and small-cap, so too the "micros" are not uniformly defined by the markets. David Evans, manager of the *Robertson-Stephens Micro-Cap Growth Fund* uses a quarter million dollars as the breakpoint to define micro-caps from within the small-cap pool of companies.[4] Jerry Edgarton of *Pathfinder Money Page* sees firms with $250 million to $1 billion as actually more like mid-cap firms, and also believes micro-caps are those miniscule companies under $250 million in market value.[5] Again, the micro-cap strategy is based on finding hidden value in areas of the market where the biggest institutional investors are not looking.

Initial Public Offers

There is also tremendous potential for growth among the dozens of initial public offers (IPO) of common stock that come to the market each quarter. Evidence suggests that underwriters deliberately underprice IPOs, compared to the eventual true market equilibrium price, in order to provide a profit incentive to the investment banks that make up the informal selling syndicate for disseminating the stock among a wide public market. During the first one to three days of the offer, prices on IPOs tend to rise very quickly to their eventual equilibrium price, as they are bid up by buyers anxious to obtain a promising growth firm. A wealth of empirical studies over the last seven decades has shown that the majority of IPOs produce very significant positive returns in the short-term. Small-cap investors should also seek to acquire emerging growth firms at this critical stage of equity investment. However, it is very difficult, if not impossible, to gain access to the earliest rounds of buying new IPO shares because the market is dominated by large institutional traders connected to the lead underwriter's selling syndicate.

The Russell 2000 Index
The Frank Russell Company provides a wide range of indexes that serve as benchmarks for the performance of various investment strategies. The Russell 2000 Index is widely regarded as perhaps the best indicator of the overall market for small-cap stocks. It measures the performance of the 2000 smallest companies that together comprise only about 10 percent of the overall Russell 3000 Index, which represents roughly 98 percent of all domestic American firms traded in the U.S. equity markets. The top 1000 companies are the largest publicly traded stocks. Companies in the Russell 2000 typically have an average market capitalization of around $470 million (the 50th percentile is around $400 million).

The Small-Cap Profile

One of the most interesting concepts related to small-cap common stocks is this: The apparently unique characteristics that set small-caps apart from mid-cap and large-cap companies (the market and financial features and prospective benefits for growth investing) also happen to be most of the major risks and concerns that can often keep investors away from this sector in the market. Many of the features that define the typical small-cap firm appear to be unique from the larger stocks on the market. Typical small-cap common stocks have the following characteristics:

1. Market capitalization is less than $1 billion.
2. The price-to-earnings multiple has generally been above 20.
3. Revenues have been quite inconsistent year to year.
4. Revenue is overconcentrated across relatively few customers.
5. Earnings generally have larger variances in the near term and long term.
6. Stock prices have high variability throughout the year.
7. Reliable information is not as readily available or accessible.
8. The beta is quite high (typically well above 1.5).
9. Trading volume tends to be low, creating a liquidity premium.
10. There are much wider bid-ask spreads during trading.
11. These firms are regular acquisition targets of large-cap firms.

There can be some difficulty in finding agreement among fund managers as to what exactly constitutes a small-cap stock, as well as other measures related to this profile list. Although individual definitions and preferences for selection will vary from manager to manager, the fact remains, the small-cap investor must understand how these concepts and characteristics relate to each other and interact with similar categorical information from mid-cap and large-cap firms in the stock markets.

Figure 2–1 presents a common tool in the market today for categorizing stocks. Notice the four groups of market capitalization on the top, and the breakpoints between each group. "Value" investing is focused on a conservative approach of buying and holding the best companies in the best industries, with the most reliable earnings. Investors who use this approach are often said to be "sticking with value" rather than speculating on relatively unproven firms. "Growth" investing moves away from the relative security of firms with proven and reliable earnings and dividends toward companies that are weighted heavier in "potential" earnings and

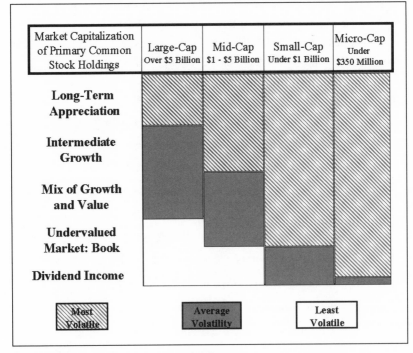

FIGURE 2–1   Investment Style Box

dividends. Where value investing looks for a solid track record of lower earnings volatility, growth investing likes to take a chance with the emerging industries and the newer firms. Some investors like to "blend" these two approaches, allowing the value to anchor the portfolio while the growth introduces an extra dose of upside potential. The highest relative risks are associated with companies of all sizes focused on long-term appreciation as well as with small-cap blended strategies. Large-cap and mid-cap value portfolios carry the lowest risk. Moderate risk is associated with blended strategies in the top two groups of stocks and value investing in small-caps. Notice that relative risks are weighted toward the small-cap companies.

Throughout this book, market capitalization will be segmented as follows: (a) small-cap firms are less than $1 billion in market capitalization, (b) mid-caps are between $1 billion and $3 billion, (c) large-caps are over $3 billion, and (d) micro-caps are firms under $300 million. The prospects for growth can be significant, so it is important to clearly define these issues, prioritize funding requirements, and set tangible objectives before investing in small-cap common stocks. The following sections discuss the details of the 11 small-cap characteristics listed on p. 21.

Under $1 Billion or Under $5 Billion?

There used to be a day when market capitalization under $1 billion meant that a company's common stock was classified as small-cap. Everything over that benchmark was considered a large-cap issue. In the past 10 to 15 years, the investment community has become more precise in its classification of publicly traded shares. Today, there is no generally accepted distinction between small-cap and large-cap stocks because two additional categories have been added to the mix. Although firms that have market capitalization over $1 billion were accepted as no longer being small-cap, many fund managers felt strongly that a majority of the issues just above this threshold still exhibited characteristics that were somewhat similar to small-cap stocks. However, as a company's market capitalization approached $3 billion, and certainly by the time the stock reached $5 billion in value, these stocks were less like small-caps and increasingly more like the largest S&P 500 firms. A new category was introduced to cover the middle-sized business transitioning from small-cap to large-cap, namely, the mid-cap stock. Most investors and finance professionals tend to agree that once a firm exceeds $1 billion in stock value it is no longer a small-cap. According to some managers, the mid-cap designation covers everything from $1 billion up to $3 billion, while for others it includes companies with capitalization as high as $5 billion.

On the opposite end of the spectrum, not all small-caps are considered entirely similar. The smallest of these have been termed micro-caps. But even with this label, there is no agreement as to where these supersmall companies begin. Many small-cap investment specialists draw the line at half a billion dollars, while some use $350 million or $400 million as the cutoff point. Empirical studies have not yet produced evidence that micro-caps are unique from the top end of the small-caps. Many mid-caps tend to behave like small-caps, others look and perform much like large-caps, and yet a good deal of research recognizes mid-caps as distinct from the smallest- and the largest-capitalized firms.

It is recommended that the small-cap investor should be thinking about companies with market values under $1 billion. These firms will require small-cap investors to perform extra research, analysis, and due diligence (speaking directly with company senior managers and customers in the industry) when considering these investments.

Price-Earnings Ratio Above 20

The price-earnings (P/E) ratio measures the market price of a stock divided by the earnings per share of the company (price over earnings). However, it is not necessarily a financial or investment measure in and of itself. Many investors love to quote the P/E of a stock as if it relays some form of company-specific information that provides insights into the nonsystematic risk of the firm. The P/E should really be thought of as an "after-measure," meaning, it merely states the relative price that investors are willing to pay for a stock based on all the available information and expectations of future performance. The question is often posed: Do investors purchase stocks based on the P/E ratio, or does the P/E ratio simply capture the expectations of investors? If the former is true, then an argument could be made that small-cap investors typically look for stocks with P/E ratios above 20 (20:1). But if the latter is true, then it could be argued that because small-cap investors have high expectations about a firm's growth, they are willing to pay prices today that are significantly higher than the company's current earnings. The fact is that both arguments are valid. Small-cap investors tend to look for stocks with relatively high P/E ratios because these companies have obviously attracted strong future expectations from those in the market. And small-cap investors tend to screen stocks that have extraordinary future earnings potential, so current prices are much higher than recent earnings. Whichever occurs first, the fact remains that small-caps, as a group, have distinctively higher P/E ratios than mid-caps and large-caps.

FORMULA

Price-Earnings Ratio =
Current Price of the Stock ÷ Current Earnings per Share

The price-earnings ratio by itself is not an indicator of a small-cap stock. There are many large-caps with very high P/E ratios. However, most small-cap stocks tend to have relatively high P/E ratios in the range of 25 to 50 because of strong investor demand based on expectations for growth. The current price is very high compared to what are generally very low current earnings per share.

Inconsistent Revenues

The typical small-cap company is still experiencing rapid, but often sporadic, growth in product and service sales. The industry is moving forward and expanding the customer base, competition may be minimal or very intense, and the small-cap firm is still learning how to maneuver through the marketplace. During one fiscal quarter, a brand-new (and very large) contract is signed and the firm's revenues grow by 35 percent. But in the subsequent quarter, a large distributor cuts orders by half because of price pressures from foreign products and the small-cap firm's revenues drop by 20 percent. The nature and interaction of an emerging industry will always be inherently volatile. Small-cap companies that compete in these environments will experience significant highs and lows in revenue performance. At the early stages of market expansion, the small-cap firm might close several large deals, but these can often be "few and far between" over the course of several fiscal years. Tremendous growth in revenues in one year can flatten out again very quickly the next, only to accelerate again as the firm gains customer recognition and implements a competitive strategy. Small-cap investors must be comfortable with inconsistent revenues, and they must look ahead to the future maturation of the company when performance will become more reliable.

Overconcentrated Revenues

The small-cap investor must also be willing to accept the increased risks associated with firms whose revenues may tend to be overly concentrated among a relatively small number of buyers. As the emerging firm develops its market strategy, it may initially secure just a half dozen or so customers who together account for more than half of the company's annual revenues. This dependence on a few clients is on the one hand a great starting point from which to build the customer base. However, on the other hand, any minor changes in order sizes or purchase cycles could dramatically affect the small-cap firm's near-term cash flow and longer-term marketing strategy. This situation can be very tenuous in the early growth stages of the small-cap firm. And yet, it can also signal a tremendous opportunity for an emerging company to experience consistently strong revenue growth as it successfully branches out from its initial sales concentration into several levels of the marketplace.

Large Variance in Earnings

Most small-cap companies also display a large variance in their earnings per share measured over the last three to five years. This variance is often even more pronounced in the shorter-term changes from one recent fiscal quarter to the next. This occurs for two reasons. First, the firm is experiencing tremendous changes in revenues as a result of the continually emerging nature of the industry. As mentioned in the preceding discussion, sales growth can be very erratic when a competitive market is expanding and new products and services are just beginning to gain widespread acceptance among customers. The second reason for the large variance in earnings is due to the disproportionate increases in both fixed overhead and variable production costs that often accompany periods of fast growth in revenues. In such a business environment, new customer orders are often flowing in at a very fast pace, but the small-cap firm generally lacks the sophisticated internal cost controls and management-operations systems to accurately monitor profitability. The result is that these companies will report fantastic earnings in the first quarter, then a decrease in earnings the next two quarters, followed by perhaps negative earnings in the fourth quarter. For the year, the firm may show an overall increase in earnings from the prior fiscal year, but the variance in earnings from year to year and within each year is typically large.

Price Volatility

The most logical outcome from the various interactions of the small-cap company's inconsistent revenues, higher P/E ratios, and larger variances in earnings is that the stock price generally experiences significant volatility in the short term, as well as during the intermediate term. This is not so much a feature to look for in a small-cap stock as it is a direct result of the way these companies are valued and traded in the market. Small-cap investors are looking for firms in rapidly developing emerging industries with the potential for extraordinary growth in revenues and subsequent profits. The attention paid to firms that fit the small-cap profile fluctuates tremendously from day to day, month to month, or quarter to quarter. This is directly related to the pace at which change occurs in various emerging industries.

Take the following example. (1) Analysis of a new technology might look very promising at first for a few select domestic industry applications. (2) But within the first fiscal year, initial products meet with less than stellar reviews. (3) Then, another firm in a different industry introduces a new process that has direct benefits to the small-cap company's product. The next generation innovation meets with initial success as joint partnerships are pursued with large distributors. (4) However, two recent modifications to an older technology have produced similar products for a few well-established firms at the top of the industry. (5) The small-cap firm then produces a third-generation product at a much lower price with the help of a manufacturing alliance. The five stages just described could happen over the course of three full years or just three fiscal quarters, depending on the pace of the changes and the response times of the firms in the industry. The point, however, is that investor attitudes about this small-cap company can vacillate rather quickly between positive and negative expectations. Heavy buying on the positive news can run the price up very fast. And a change of heart by investors because of some recent news can just as quickly cause the stock to drop. Although much of the historical evidence presented in the next chapter points to very favorable long-term performance among small-cap companies, the short-term volatility week to week and quarter by quarter makes many investors hesitant to place these stocks in their portfolio.

Information Gaps

There is a noticeable lack of consistent and reliable information pertaining to most small-cap stocks. The typical small-cap firm is many times a relatively new entrant to the industry, and even newer to the public stock market. The company might also have only a regional, or even subregional, reputation for its products and services. Most of the third-party reporting agencies, such as the *Moody's Industrial Manual*, the *Standard & Poor's Stock Guide*, and the *Value Line Investment Survey*, tend to focus their analysis on the larger companies that are more well known in their respective industries and have national name recognition throughout the investment community. Small-cap stocks are generally described as "ignored," "overlooked," and "lesser known." This does not mean that there is nothing available on these firms or that the large institutional fund managers purposely ignore or overlook these lesser-known stocks. But the top tier of investment professionals in the market pay much closer attention to large national and multinational companies, often emphasizing value or dividend income over growth objectives. Small-cap investors might be hard pressed to locate good sources for company-specific information about production, marketing strategies, firm competition, pending partnership deals, and senior management decisions.

However, this information gap, which is one of the drawbacks to small-cap investing, also serves as one of the best incentives to invest in such companies. Small-cap investors look very favorably on this lack of general knowledge in the market because they believe that they can gain a distinct advantage through highly focused research and intensive analysis. An exhaustive due diligence might produce exclusive information about the company's prospects that could reward investors with extraordinary stock returns over the long term. Whether this can be accomplished systematically is not clear. Chapter 4 will examine the topic of fundamental analysis and how it relates to market efficiency and the process of examining emerging industries in search of high-growth potential small-cap stocks.

High Beta

The previous chapter discussed the risk-return trade-off associated with investment objectives. In assessing the relative risk of a stock, the contemporary investment community uses the beta coefficient developed by Bill Sharpe in the 1960s (Figure 1–1). Beta is simply a ratio of any stock's covariance with the market (the numerator) divided by the variance of the market alone (the denominator). The fully diversified market portfolio of stocks (the denominator) serves as a good measure of an "average" level of risk. The numerator is either smaller than the market variance (beta less than 1), the same as the market variance (beta right at 1), or larger than the market variance (beta greater than 1). All individual stocks traded in the public markets are individually compared over a running 60-month window of time to calculate beta. The S&P 500 Index typically serves as the measure of the average market risk. If a stock's monthly returns tend to vary with similar size and direction (negative or positive) compared to the broad market, then the beta ratio will be around 1 and the stock is considered to have a variance similar to the overall market. Small-cap stocks tend to have unusually high betas (much greater than 1). As with the P/E, beta is not so much a thing to look for in a small-cap stock but a result of volatile revenues and profits in a very erratic but emerging industry.

RESEARCH TIP

Small-cap stocks with high betas are not always good investments. Just because a company has a high beta does not mean it will outperform the broader market. A high beta simply means that, historically (over the last 60 months), a stock has been more volatile than movement in the underlying market. This may mean greater upside movement in an "up" market, but it also means greater downside movement in a "bear" market.

Low Trading Volume

Another prominent small-cap characteristic deals with the decreased trading activity that takes place in the stock during an average day or week compared to the larger companies listed on the various stock markets. Unlike the big firms that have readily liquid markets with many buyers and sellers for shares (including market makers employed by the exchanges), the small-caps typically do not generate the same level of trading volume and are subject to significantly less activity among brokers. This can significantly reduce the ability of the small-cap investor to either find shares that are available to buy or to sell shares in a timely manner. This reduced liquidity contributes additional risk to the small-cap portfolio.

Wider Bid-Ask Spread

The last characteristic deals with the size of the dollar difference between what a buyer is willing to pay for a share (the bid price of the stock) and a seller is asking for the stock. This difference is called the bid-ask spread. A narrow spread means that the buyers' (those wanting to acquire shares) opinion about the correct price for each share is very similar to that of the sellers' opinion. When reliable information about individual companies abounds, everyone is trading on virtually identical data and the bid-ask spread is narrow. But when information is not as readily available or closely watched by traders and analysts, the spread widens, reflecting the disparity in information about the stock's true price. *The Wall Street Journal*, *Investor's Business Daily*, and other stock market periodicals report the price of the first trade of the day, the highest-priced trade for the day, the lowest-priced trade, and the last trade for the day. But they do not report the actual bid-ask spread that was present among the actual traders in the stocks. Investors will find a much wider spread between what buyers and sellers think small-cap stocks are worth. This can work to the advantage of the buyer, who can bid much lower than the current asking prices, but it can also work against the seller, who wants what appears to be a much higher price per share.

Regular Takeover Targets

Small-cap stocks make great acquisitions for mid-size and large-cap firms because they are companies that typically have one strong competency in a particular product, manufacturing process, or technology application, and they have made a significant impact as one of the leaders in an emerging market. Larger firms that are more widely diversified in their product and service offerings view the name recognition and initial customer loyalty developed by the small-cap firm as excellent value and a means for the large company to either enter this newly found industry or broaden the scope of its competitive position using the small-cap acquisition as a complement to its initial foray into the marketplace.

Notes

1. Greenwald, John, 1998. "Crazy Stock Ride," *Time*, July 20, p. 43.

2. "The Business Week Global 1000," 1998. *Business Week*, July 13, pp.70–84.

3. Weber, Joseph, 1998. "The Year of the Deal," *Business Week*, July 13, pp. 52–53.

4. *Mutual Funds Magazine Online*, www.mfmag.com, July 8, 1998.

5. Edgarton, Jerry, 1998. "Winning Funds That Fish for Small Stocks," *Pathfinder Money Page*, www.pathfinder.com, July 8.

CHAPTER 3

The Small-Cap Track Record: Historical Evidence

T here exists a great deal of controversy in the markets today as to whether there really is an extraordinary performance premium attributable to small-cap stocks. Perhaps one of the most celebrated studies in support of small-cap stocks is the now famous University of Chicago doctoral dissertation written by Rolf Banz that was published in 1981. He concluded that small-cap stocks had steadily outperformed large-cap stocks for the 50-plus years between 1926 and 1979, and he showed that issues from smaller firms generated large positive returns, especially during the periods 1931–1935 and 1941–1945.[1] This study has proved to be an oft-heard rallying cry from Wall Street fund managers trying to attract investment capital to their small-cap specialty funds. And yet many other studies have found that, for various time periods, small-cap stocks have actually underperformed mid-cap and large-cap stocks. For example, between 1979 and 1998, the Russell 2000 Small-Cap Index declined in 86 of those 231 months (37 percent of the time), with an average monthly drop of -3.9 percent in down months. During the same period, the Russell Mid-Cap Index declined in only 66 of the 231 months (28 percent of the time), with an average monthly drop of just -2.8 percent.[2] And while small-caps funds had a recent 12-month return of 36.11 percent (May 7, 1997 to May 7, 1998) versus a 32.29 percent return in large-cap funds, the very same large-caps had an average annual return of 19.04 percent for the prior *five* years (May 1993 to May 1998) versus 18.34 percent for small-caps.[3] It is very important for the small-cap investor to understand the full range of evidence pertaining to small-cap stocks and utilize a strategy that recognizes the best approaches for including small-cap companies in portfolio allocation and investment planning.

The Good News

The good news is that there are plenty of small-cap stocks to choose from, and their track record does offer great potential for investing today and in the future. The Pensions and Investments research group examined the small-cap effect for the 70 years from 1926 to 1996. They broke all the NYSE stocks into 10 groups (from the largest to smallest market capitalizations), adding AMEX stocks in 1963 and NASDAQ issues in 1975. The smallest 10 percent of the companies had an average annual return premium of 8.26 percent versus the largest 10 percent in the group. Table 3–1 summarizes these performance findings.[4] The smallest 20 percent had an average annual return premium of between 3.5 and 6.5 percent versus either the largest 10 percent, the top 20 percent, the top 30 percent, or the top 40 percent of the stocks.

TABLE 3–1   Performance by Market Capitalization Groups (1926–1996)

Market Capitalization	Average Annual Return (%)
Largest 10% of stocks	11.56%
Next largest (80th percentile)	13.50%
Next largest (70th percentile)	13.75%
Next largest (60th percentile)	14.67%
Next largest (50th percentile)	15.44%
Next largest (40th percentile)	15.11%
Next largest (30th percentile)	16.15%
Next largest (20th percentile)	16.41%
2nd smallest (10th percentile)	17.08%
Smallest 10% of stocks	19.82%

Great Expectations
Great ideas for products, creative approaches to problem solving, and innovative solutions to business issues are key factors for successful small-cap investing. The opportunity to provide equity capital to an emerging company, just as it is ready to make a significant impact in a competitive industry, is still the foundation of the small-cap investment program. The facts are plain and simple: Significant gains in value accrue to investors who have the vision to look far ahead of the contemporary market and recognize a well-positioned company either leading an emerging trend or providing support for new products and services at the forefront of such a trend. Many such firms just happen to be smaller, entrepreneurial firms that are highly innovative and creative and able to quickly adapt to changes that occur in their competitive industry. A five-year-old company with market capitalization of $600 million, a great management team, and a super product group that is leading a significant industry change will probably generate substantial positive abnormal returns to those investors who were already shareholders before the recent round of growth commenced.

Questions About Performance

Jeremy Siegel has argued that an anomaly took place with small-caps during 1975 to 1983, and that if this period is not counted in the long-term performance of small-cap stocks, their returns are no longer significant when compared to large-cap stocks.[5] But, that does not completely undercut the small-cap findings of Banz because his data are from 1926 to 1979, and the relatively short period of 1975–1979 is not enough to completely bias his overall conclusion that favored small-cap stocks over large-cap companies. Refer back to the 70 years presented in Table 3–1. Even if the 1926 to 1996 period excludes returns earned during 1975–1983 (as suggested by Siegel), there is still a small-cap premium even after adjusting for the eight years of 1975 to 1983. Table 3–2 shows the average annual returns for the same combined NYSE, AMEX, and NASDAQ groupings based on market capitalization for the entire period of 1926 to 1996, excluding 1975–1983, and then the returns just for the period 1975 to 1983.[4] Granted, the eight years of growth from 1975 to 1983 were extraordinary, but the entire market enjoyed a strong and prolonged expansion. Many new companies were introduced and numerous emerging industries were birthed during this pivotal juncture of American private enterprise development in communication systems, electronics technologies, and information systems. That period should not be removed but instead further underscores the significant contribution of small-cap firms to capital market growth. And even with that period removed, an annual small-cap premium of between 3.1 and 6.49 percent still exists between the smallest 10 percent of firms and the largest 10 percent of firms, as well as the smallest 20 percent and all combinations of groups above the 60th percentile.

TABLE 3–2   Adjusted Performance by Market Capitalization Groups

| | Average Annual Return (%) | |
Market Capitalization	1926–1996 (excl. '75–'83)	1975–1983 Alone
Largest 10% of stocks	11.01%	14.84%
Next largest (>80th percentile)	12.64%	19.42%
Next largest (>70th percentile)	12.37%	23.21%
Next largest (>60th percentile)	12.93%	26.64%
Next largest (>50th percentile)	13.82%	26.63%
Next largest (>40th percentile)	13.19%	28.31%
Next largest (>30th percentile)	14.11%	30.23%
Next largest (>20th percentile)	14.23%	31.37%
2nd smallest (>10th percentile)	14.84%	32.53%
Smallest 10% of stocks	17.50%	35.84%

Some researchers have suggested that market capitalization is a close proxy for other "size" criteria, such as the book value of the firm's assets and the level of sales revenues. Table 3–3 compares all stocks listed on the New York Stock Exchange for the 20 years between 1967 and 1987, broken down into 10 portfolios, first based on the largest market capitalization firms down through the smallest, and then using book value of the firm's assets and sales revenues. The figures presented are the proceeds of one dollar invested in each of the 10 portfolios across each of the three categories by which firm size might be defined.[6] Notice that the smallest firms produced the largest returns in all three size categories, but the disparity between the smallest firms and the largest firms was most pronounced based upon market capitalization, with a spread differential of nearly $33 ($40.51 compared to $7.30). And the spreads from smallest to largest (based upon book value of assets) were around $13 ($22.99 vs. $9.95), and a little over $8 based upon size of sales revenues ($18.44 vs. $10.17).

TABLE 3–3   Stock Performance for Every One Dollar Invested (1967–1987)

Portfolio Size	Market Cap	Book Value	Sales
Top 10% largest firms	$ 7.30	$ 9.95	$10.17
Second 10th of firms	8.81	12.53	13.82
Third 10th of firms	9.62	11.33	12.28
Fourth 10th of firms	9.06	9.83	10.22
Fifth 10th of firms	11.41	13.39	17.38
Sixth 10th of firms	14.86	14.34	12.57
Seventh 10th of firms	11.53	14.42	12.24
Eighth 10th of firms	18.93	15.55	14.59
Ninth 10th of firms	21.63	16.04	18.33
Smallest 10% of firms	$40.51	$22.99	$18.44

There were no perfectly consistent identifiable patterns throughout any of the three categories of stocks when moving sequentially from the largest companies to the smallest. Among those segmented by market capitalization, the fourth level had smaller returns than the third, and the seventh level had smaller returns than the sixth. However, this might be due to the lack of clearly defined breakpoints between firm sizes, and perhaps the top four levels might represent large-cap stocks, the fifth through seventh levels mid-cap companies, and the bottom three levels the small-cap firms. When each of the three categories is plotted on a graph, showing the 10 groups on the horizontal axis and proceeds on the vertical axis, there is no significant trend for either the book value or sales revenues groups. But, there is a very significant *upward* sloping line for the market capitalization category, such that the smaller the firm's market capitalization, the larger its overall returns.

Following up on the previous results, the same stocks were also sorted into five levels, first by book value of the firm's assets and sales revenues and then by market capitalization within each level.[6] Table 3–4 shows each of the five levels of book value on the left and market cap across the top. The highest returns were earned among the smallest market caps at each level except the third. When they were next sorted by market cap first and then book value within each level, the highest returns were consistently earned among the smallest market caps. Next, they were sorted first by sales revenues, then by market cap within each level, and the highest returns were again consistently earned by the smallest market caps in each sales level. And finally, they were sorted first by market cap and then by sales, and the highest returns were once again, across-the-board, earned by the smallest market cap levels.

This highlights both the inconsistencies of how "size" is defined and the strong support for market capitalization as a significant measure of a company's stock-return potential, even when certain breakpoints for large-cap, mid-cap, and small-cap may not be perfectly defined on a level-by-level basis.

FORMULA

Book Value = Company Net Worth ÷ Common Shares Outstanding

A firm's book value is based on the combined value of the common stock par value, any paid-in-capital (funds in excess of the offering price raised at the IPO), and cumulative retained earnings. It represents the balance sheet equity (excluding any preferred stock), which is essentially the difference between the value of the firm's assets and its outstanding debt. Book value per share is then this net worth spread over the number of common shares outstanding.

The Neglected Stock Effect

Many securities analysts argue that the entire basis for the extraordinary returns apparently available in small-cap companies is due to a general lack of interest, research, and consistent monitoring of smaller firms by the financial community.[7] Much of the original work focused on smaller samples of stocks from the 1970s and early 1980s that were taken from the S&P 500 Index (not exactly an appropriate test of the small-cap effect). Recent and more comprehensive studies have shown that when stocks

TABLE 3–4   The Relationship of Market Value, Book Value, Asset Value, and Sales Revenues with Highest Returns on Stocks

Book Values	Market Capitalization				
	Largest	**4th**	**3rd**	**2nd**	**Smallest Firms**
Largest					**Highest returns**
4th					**Highest**
3rd			Highest		—
2nd					**Highest**
Smallest					**Highest**

Market Cap	Book Value of Assets				
	Largest	**4th**	**3rd**	**2nd**	**Smallest Assets**
Largest					
4th					
3rd					
2nd					
Smallest firms	**Highest**	**Highest**	**Highest**	**Highest**	**Highest returns**

Sales	Market Capitalization				
	Largest	**4th**	**3rd**	**2nd**	**Smallest Firms**
Largest					**Highest returns**
4th					**Highest returns**
3rd					**Highest returns**
2nd					**Highest returns**
Smallest					**Highest returns**

Market Cap	Sales Revenues				
	Largest	**4th**	**3rd**	**2nd**	**Smallest**
Largest					
4th					
3rd					
2nd					
Smallest firms	**Highest**	**Highest**	**Highest**	**Highest**	**Highest returns**

are sorted based on the degree of neglect they experience among securities analysts, they are also essentially sorted based on their market capitalization. Table 3–5 summarizes findings based upon more than 7000 stocks from the NYSE, the AMEX, and the NASDAQ from January 1982 through December 1995, where stocks were ranked as either highly neglected, moderately neglected, moderately followed, or highly followed. Notice that the "highly neglected" stocks had returns that were not all that different from the "moderately neglected," "moderately followed," and "highly followed" stocks for the top six levels of market capitalization. But, based upon the 14 years of average returns and the variances in each category, the highest returns were consistently earned among the four smallest levels of market caps for the unique group consisting of highly neglected stocks. In all other sizes of market capitalization, there were no differences between neglected or followed stocks. This points once again to the notion that stock returns must be more closely related to the small-cap effect, rather than the lack of a unified research and analysis by large institutional investors and the greater financial community at large.

TABLE 3–5   Stock Followings, Market Capitalization, and Average Annual Returns (Jan. 1982–Dec. 1995)

	Market Capitalization									
Level of Neglect	**Smallest 10%**	**2nd**	**3rd**	**4th**	**5th**	**6th**	**7th**	**8th**	**9th**	**Largest 10%**
Highly neglected	56.7%	31.3	25.7	25.7	19.2*	13.8	14.5	17.2	14.2	—
Moderately neglected	31.1%	16.1	20.3	17.8	14.4	16.4	12.5	15.5	—	—
Moderately followed	—	30.2	14.3	20.2	14.9	16.1	16.5	17.3	14.8	10.9
Closely followed	—	—	—	—	17.6*	16.1	16.4	16.5	16.7	16.6

*Note: Although the highly neglected average return was higher, the variances in returns were all very large in the 5th level of market capitalization, and there was no significance related to being "highly neglected."

The January Effect

For most of the 1970s and 1980s there was a good deal of discussion and analysis dealing with the so-called turn-of-the-year, or January, effect among stock returns.[8] The supposed anomaly went something like this: Investors who purchased stocks right at the end of December/beginning of January, would realize extraordinarily high returns in the first few weeks of the new year. Several studies have challenged the notion of making excess returns in this one month, usually attributing such returns to large volume end-of-year tax-loss selling by portfolio managers.[9] The quest for a rational, fundamental explanation of this enigma has gained recent support in the idea that the risk of small-cap stocks does not remain constant throughout the year, so that small-cap investors require a higher rate of return for their risk assumed in January, and these so-called extraordinary returns are actually quite normal and right in line with the risk-return expectations at the start of the year.[10] There is still no overwhelming evidence that the small-cap effect captures other underlying market or trading phenomenon. The systematic extraordinary returns earned in small-cap stocks mean there will remain several on-going challenges to the integrity of the small-cap investment strategy.

The "Small" January Effect?

This phenomenon has been widely studied by financial researchers for decades. Most professionals accept the fact that it probably captures a "size effect" and does not reveal a year-end timing opportunity for common stocks. Smaller firms tend to have greater upside potential for price appreciation. Although small-caps are often eagerly sought by investors at the start of the new calendar year, there is no basis to believe that they will systematically gain in value during the month of January.

"Real" Small-Cap Investing

The truth is, there is no clear definition of what constitutes a great small-cap stock, and there is no evidence that guarantees that small-cap stocks will consistently outperform mid-cap and large-cap stocks over any given time period. Several of the unique features of small-cap stocks do contribute to increased volatility and perhaps a decrease in liquidity and information impacts when compared with stocks from larger firms. And, as with any investment, the historical performance of one small-cap stock or a certain small-cap fund cannot serve as an indicator of future positive returns. There are two key conclusions to take from the evidence just presented in this chapter. First, all in all, small-cap stocks have shown tremendous gains at various time periods over the last several decades, and these returns have, in many cases, far outpaced the traditional benchmarks of performance such as the Dow Jones Industrial Average and the S&P 500 Index. But the second conclusion is much more critical to the understanding of how to be a successful small-cap investor: *Extraordinary growth is not unique to small-cap companies*. Many mid-cap and large-cap firms also experience significant positive abnormal returns because of market share and sales growth in their industry that is due to cutting-edge product and service innovations. In the same context, not all small-cap firms are poised for tremendous growth either. There is no correlation between the size of a company's market capitalization and its ability to successfully introduce winning ideas to its industry. Just as there are many large-cap and mid-cap firms that will not experience huge gains in corporate earnings and share value because they are not positioned to capitalize on the hottest trend(s) in their industry.

The following chapter will examine the process of identifying new markets for small-cap investing, by systematically researching and following the latest business trends and the most promising of the newly emerging industries. Whether the small-cap phenomenon can be explained by other underlying fundamental factors or it is a true investment enigma that warrants serious inquiry remains the decision that portfolio managers must deal with when searching for excellent opportunities among the thousands of common stocks that trade in the public markets every day. The small-cap performance track record is impressive and merits a thorough investigation by investors.

Notes

1.   Banz, Rolf W., 1981. "The Relationship Between Return and Market Value of Common Stocks," *Journal of Financial Economics*, Volume 9, March, pp. 23–37.

2. Lipper Analytical Services, Inc.. www.lipperweb.com.

3. Ibid.

4. Booth, David G., 1997. "The 'Small-Cap Effect,' by Some Accounts, is a Myth," *Dimensional Fund Advisors, Inc.*, February, pp. 1–2.

5. Siegel, Jeremy, 1997. "The 'Small-Cap Effect:' by Some Accounts a Myth," *The Wall Street Journal*, February 10, pp. C–1; C–6.

6. Berk, Jonathan B., 1997. "Does Size Really Matter?" *Financial Analysts Journal*, September–October, pp. 12–18.

7. See such works as: Arbel and Strebel, 1982. "The Neglected and Small-Firm Effects," *Financial Review*, November, pp. 201–218; and 1983, "Pay Attention to Neglected Firms," *Journal of Portfolio Management*, Winter, pp. 37–42; Lo and MacKinlay, 1990. "Data-Snooping Biases in Tests of Asset Pricing Models," *Review of Financial Studies*, Fall, pp. 431–467; Beard and Sias, 1997. "Is There a Neglected-Firm Effect?" *Financial Analysts Journal*, September–October, pp. 19–23.

8. See Keim, Don, 1983. "Size Related Anomalies and Stock Return Seasonality," *Journal of Financial Economics*, June, pp. 13–32; Barges, McConnell, and Schlarbaum, 1984. "An Investigation of the Turn-of-the-Year Effects," *Journal of Finance*, Number 39, pp. 185–192; or the 1983 special issue of the *Journal of Financial Economics*, "Symposium on Size and Stock Returns and Other Empirical Irregularities," June.

9. See Madrick, James, 1977. "Shooting Holes in the January Indicator," *Business Week*, January 31, p. 71; Hulbert, Michael, 1987. "The January Indicator: Case Against It Still Stands," *American Association of Individual Investors Newsletter*, January, pp. 20–22; or Ritter, Jay, 1988. "The Buying and Selling Behavior of Individual Investors at the Turn of the Year," *Journal of Finance*, July, pp. 701–717.

10. Rogalski and Tinic, 1986. "The January Size Effect: Anomaly or Risk Measurement?" *Financial Analysts Journal*, November–December, pp. 63–70.

Investor's Toolbox

4

Identifying
Emerging Industries

Here is absolutely no way to know for sure where the next great growth industry will appear in business. Hindsight is wonderful. It allows investors to sit around and talk about the companies that have already achieved rapid growth in sales, outstanding product and service penetration in an industry, and huge increases in the stock's price. What small-cap investor wouldn't like to look back on the portfolio and see Compaq Computer purchased in 1984? Were there clear signals in 1983 that Compaq was poised for phenomenal long-term growth? The continuously emerging Internet is another example of a major industry that is creating incredible opportunities for both "hot" new ventures and small-cap investors wanting to participate in the growth of this technology and marketplace. Many businesses today are establishing exclusive marketing partnerships, such as the recent agreement between The Motley Fool Investment Group and Amazon.com, Incorporated. Disney purchased a 43 percent stake in recent Internet start-up Infoseek for more than $1 billion.[1] And Netscape rebounded significantly from around $15 in early 1998 to more than $36 per share on news that Time Warner would make an offer to acquire the company.[2] Small-cap investors who can stay focused and up to date with these kinds of emerging industry trends can position their stock portfolios to profit from the potential growth of all kinds of new ideas and business systems.

The reality is that today there are many small-cap firms available for portfolio inclusion that will not achieve significant capital appreciation in share price over the next four-to-six years. And, of course, there are numerous small-caps, sitting on a stockpile of hidden value, that are poised to make a huge impact in their respective product or service markets. This chapter is focused on developing a systematic approach to screening current and prospective business trends as they relate to the basic three tiers of fundamental analysis: (1) macroeconomic information, (2) industry-level information, and (3) microeconomic firm-level information. This model cannot guarantee small-cap investment success, but it can provide a clear process by which investment opportunities can be identified and decided upon.

Classic Fundamental Analysis

Perhaps no other topic in investment finance is considered to be as basic to the *expected* value of a firm than what has been termed *fundamental analysis*. In fact, today, all professionals in the investments and portfolio management industry clearly reside in one of two camps with respect to the function of firm valuation. These camps are either the fundamental approach or the technical approach, and by far, the vast majority of Wall Street adheres to the fundamental side of the fence when it comes to firm value. There are no exact figures published anywhere, but it is generally presumed that less than 10 percent of investment managers subscribe to the tenets of technical analysis for firm valuation.

Market Efficiency

Small-cap investors interested in screening public companies for potential hidden value must have a basic understanding of how information is thought to influence stock prices. Modern Portfolio Theory (MPT) is built on several core assumptions. One very important and foundational premise deals with whether or not the market operates in an "efficient" manner. What does that mean? If stock prices move in a *random* fashion that is completely unrelated to their previous historical price levels, the market is efficient, because no one would be able to profit from knowing the recent price behavior. And that makes sense, because everyone in the market has access to the exact same historical stock price information, so how could anyone use that to their advantage when investing? Those who hold to this basic notion of market efficiency believe that the price of a stock is a function of fundamental information about the firm and other related economic issues. Those who reject market efficiency believe that the price of a stock is a function of its historical price movements and patterns. These are "technical" factors, and are entirely different than news about the firm, its industry, and the general economy.

Are Markets Efficient?

Market efficiency has been debated and researched for over 40 years. The main argument essentially states that if past price patterns are an indicator of future price performance, then the market is inefficient and price movements are nonrandom. If past prices are not indicators of future price movements, the market is weak-form efficient, and price movements are random. But not all public information may be reflected in the price, so research could provide insights for investors to improve their portfolio performance. But if all public information is available to everyone, no investor should be able to benefit from analyzing it. In this case the markets are considered semistrong form efficient, and only private (insider) information is not reflected in the price. However, if even private information is already reflected in the price, the markets are strong-form efficient. The vast majority of the contemporary investment-finance community holds that the stock market is at least weak-form efficient, and probably leans toward exhibiting some semistrong form efficiency characteristics. The fact that many portfolio managers outperform the market each year means that the market is probably not strong-form efficient.

Technical Versus Fundamental Analysis

In short, the technical side of the industry holds that markets are inherently inefficient. This means they believe that prior price movements of a publicly traded financial security serve as indicators of the future price. This is built upon an underlying assumption that prices move in a decidedly *non*random fashion, and as such, the record keeping and charting of historical price movements will reveal various readily identifiable patterns that serve as indicators of future price performance. On the other hand, the fundamental side of the industry holds that markets are, at the very least, weak-form efficient. This means they believe that at the very least (the "weakest" form of market efficiency) prior price movements exhibit no indications about the level of the future price of a stock. The underlying assumption is that prices move in a decidedly *random* manner, and as such, charting historical price movements is a fruitless endeavor that will reveal absolutely nothing about future prices. There are two other positions in the fundamental camp dealing with this concept of market efficiency.

Figure 4–1 outlines the relationship between the fundamental and technical sides of the investment industry and the three progressive categories within the fundamental position. Notice that the key dividing point is where an investor moves from the technical side of the house, where prices are believed to move in specific nonrandom patterns, to the fundamental side of the house, where prices are believed to move in a completely random manner. Those to the left of the dotted line assume the market is inefficient, while those to the right of the line hold that the market is at least weak-form efficient. At this first stage, investors accept that stock prices move in a random fashion, but they also believe that not all of the available public information pertaining to the firm is reflected in the share

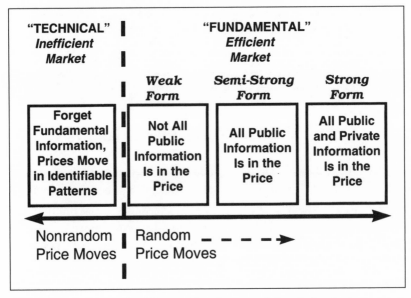

FIGURE 4–1   Technical Versus Fundamental Stock Analysis

price. So, a small-cap investor who holds to a "weak" form of efficiency believes that diligent research and analysis into a company are worthwhile, because there is information out there that could be uncovered that has not yet been considered by investors.

Some investors on the fundamental side of the fence would move even a bit further to the right and state that stock prices not only move in a random fashion but also reflect all of the available public information. This is called the *semistrong form of market efficiency*. This means that even after completing thorough research and analysis, anything an investor could uncover about a firm in the available public information has already been factored into the share's price by other investors in the market. Essentially, this means there is no reward for doing homework on a company, because every other investor has also looked at the exact same information, and this has already been factored into the stock price. The only insight not reflected in the existing price is private *insider* information. This is the confidential, proprietary knowledge that the senior executives have about the firm's financial, marketing, managerial, and operational strategies. An investor could then benefit from obtaining this private information because it is outside the realm of the available public information.

The most extreme position on the fundamental side of common stock valuation holds that even the private insider information has been taken into consideration by all of the buyers and sellers in the market. This is referred to as the *strong-form of efficiency*. There are very few adherents to this position, because if it were true, there would be no way to profit from owning common stocks, because every piece of information available (both public and insider) would already be included in the current price level. The investment incentive to do research and then purchase common stocks would be completely removed.

Macroeconomic Information

The "big picture" effect in valuing small-cap stocks always begins with the condition of the overall macro economy. Numerous factors are assembled about the state of the nation's productivity, cash flow, and business dealings with other countries, and when reviewed in their entirety, these measures provide insights into the overall health of the American enterprise system. There is little consensus among economists as to which factors provide the most accurate assessments of the economy's current and future strength, but several factors are considered basic fundamentals in this first tier of analysis. Typically, most securities analysts keep tabs on the following key macroeconomic factors:

1. The index of leading economic indicators
2. Federal Reserve monetary policy
3. The level of interest rates for borrowing
4. The nation's employment figures
5. Producer and consumer price inflation
6. Federal government spending policies
7. The nation's foreign trade balances
8. The nation's gross domestic product

The macro economy sets the tone for a generally favorable or unfavorable business climate. There are certainly many other macroeconomic factors that are tallied and monitored, but these eight areas represent the core of the first tier in fundamental stock analysis. The status of the national economy sets the tone for future expectations across the range of industries that comprise American private enterprise. Investor sentiment gets its start at this first tier. Optimism bodes well for industry and firm forecasts, while pessimism can signal a reluctance among investors to buy stocks.

INDUSTRY INFORMATION

Having gauged the big picture, fundamental analysis turns its attention to the health of the specific industry in which a company does business. Today, some of the more popular industries to watch include: bio-medical technologies, computer hardware, computer software, wireless telecommunications, pharmaceuticals, automobiles, and aerospace electronics. The industry outlook is pulled in two directions. It is many times a function of both the macro economy in one direction and the condition of the firms in the particular industry in the other direction. So the question is often posed, Does fundamental industry analysis draw its course from the nature of the macroeconomic analysis, or does individual company analysis set the tone for the industry outlook? Certainly there is some truth to the latter, that a few key firms making great strides in product and service innovations can establish a favorable basis for a given industry. And this can recycle back to other, less prominent firms in the industry, providing a second round of optimism for that sector of the economy. Many industries find their initial success concentrated among a small handful of successful firms, and this rebounds back at a later date to include the balance of the companies in that industry as well. And yet many fundamental analysts hold that the industry gains its momentum from the other direction: Namely, that the tone of the macro economy fuels the expectations at the industry level. The small-cap investor must recognize the industry's place in the national outlook as well as each company's potential contribution to the projected health of the industry.

Figure 4–2 summarizes the relative positioning of industry analysis with respect to macroeconomic and company-specific information. A particular new product or service innovation does not necessarily have to be based in a certain type of macro economy.

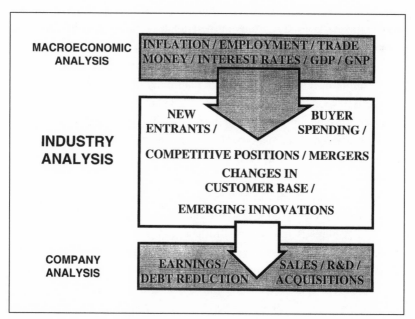

FIGURE 4–2 **Macroeconomic, Industry, and Company Analysis**

The status of a breakthrough product technology or a newly developed manufacturing process is not dependent upon a certain level of interest rates, monetary policy, national employment, or inflation.   Great ideas come to fruition in all kinds of economic settings. Research and development efforts are not gauged by the typical business cycles. When a new concept is ready for the market, the industry is generally configured around one or two pioneering firms, and many others who quickly stake a claim to various niches and clientele. Good fundamental industry analysis is focused on the emergence of sound ideas that translate into highly marketable products and services.

COMPANY INFORMATION

The third tier of fundamental analysis focuses squarely on the individual firms that comprise an industry. Firm-specific analysis identifies the nonsystematic risks unique to a company's products, services, competitive positioning, market share, senior executives and general management talent, research and development potential, and financial situation.[3] It is at this level that most small-cap investors believe the "hidden value" resides. Small-cap firms may have fantastic new products or services to bring to the market or a pending partnership deal with a large distributor in the industry. Emerging companies may have joint research and development contracts with government agencies or multinational marketing firms. A firm might have a patent pending on a highly innovative new technology that will soon go into full production. Their owner-entrepreneur may be poised to sign a long-term deal to supply a huge aerospace conglomerate with a brand-new technology. This firm-specific information is deemed very valuable and certainly worth the efforts of exhaustive research and analysis.

As was the case with industry analysis, the question is often asked, Does a strong industry bode well for the potential of any given individual firm in that industry, or do firms initiate and generate and sustain what ultimately becomes the strong position of a given industry? The small-cap investor has to decide whether a great industry can exist on its own, and, as such, support great companies. Or perhaps extraordinary firms perform well on their own, and then provide the industry with credibility and optimism among investors.

Five Important Industry Characteristics

The industry analysis is wedged between the macroeconomic news and the potential performance of individual firms. But the small-cap investor must begin the stock selection process at the industry level. The pool of prospective companies should be drawn from among the very best ventures in the very best industries. And the industry will either have emerging growth characteristics or not. There are probably dozens of variables that could qualify an industry as being truly "emerging." The following section discusses five specific characteristics that should be well represented in the industries being considered by small-cap investors. These are: (1) the application scope, (2) the product or service orientation, (3) the concentration impact, (4) the compatibility factor, and (5) the competitive density of external market environment. It is certainly not an exhaustive list, but it can used as a highly selective tool in the critique of so-called emerging industries and help investors determine where to hunt for potential small-cap growth stocks.

Application Scope

The first signals of an emerging industry are captured by what is called potency contribution. Two characteristics, the "everyday life" factor and consumer orientation, fall under this heading. Although they are closely related, they are not the same thing. Everyday life describes the normal fit of the products and services coming out of an industry. When an innovation is applicable to a major component of the typical day of the average person, it has an everyday-life focus. This is quite different from the product or service concept that is limited to only specific uses in a narrow market niche. Small-cap investors should first qualify an industry's potency using this measure. For example, there are many new ideas that come to the market that have applications in virtually every business office from California to New York. Or there are products, which can work in any home, school, or hospital, that will save money, do things more efficiently, or provide benefits that were not available with existing products. The wider the everyday application, the greater the market potential and the better the prospects for company sales growth and profitability.

Product Orientation

The second potency signal defines the product or service orientation as a consumer focus, a wholesale-supplier emphasis, a capital and manufacturing target, or an office-management orientation. An industry positioned to take advantage of significant consumer demand may be viewed as much stronger than a wholesale, or original equipment manufacturer, industry. Some segments of product orientation have much greater potential for industry sales than others. In many cases, consumer-oriented industries offer the greatest industry strength because of the sheer numbers of potential individual buyers available in both domestic and related foreign markets. Figure 4–3 outlines the relationship between the application scope and the product's market orientation for an emerging industry. Notice that the greatest potential for industry impact generally comes from products and services that are expected to be ubiquitous in the marketplace. These are consumer-oriented markets that have everyday life applications. Both the specialty and prominent product-service groups provide moderate industry potential, while narrowly targeted niche offerings present the least potential for industry growth.

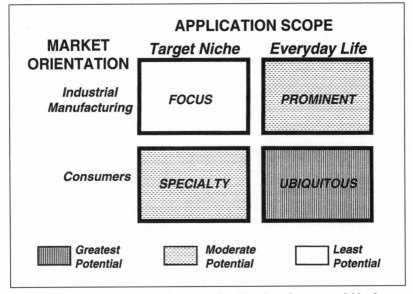

FIGURE 4–3   Industry Analysis by Application Scope and Market Orientation

Concentration Impact

The strongest growth industries are characterized by several tiers of both providers and users. These tiers are generally a function of: (a) cost (or price), (b) different configurations of features, and (c) overall quality and service. The industry is most healthy when it has the potential to accommodate several layers of firms, rather than just a few similar companies.

The greater the response in the industry through many combinations of costs (prices), features, and quality, the more efficiently market competition is dispersed across numerous types of products and companies. The concentration impact measures the depth and breadth of the industry. Again, as with the application scope and orientation, the industries with the greatest growth potential have a comprehensive range of products or services (all kinds of prices, features, and quality levels) and the widest reach to varied buyer groups.

Compatibility

An industry will either be linked with other compatible products and complementary industries or it will be somewhat isolated as a "stand-alone space" in the business environment. These can either be *direct* links, where the product or service is designed specifically to work in conjunction with existing technologies, features, and platforms; or they can be *indirect* links, where the product or service has interaction with secondary (once removed) or tertiary (twice removed) technologies, perhaps as a component part or as a service add-on feature. The best small-cap companies will at least have a few strong indirect links, and probably numerous excellent direct links, with significant product and service areas in the industry. This helps to assure the small company of a position relative to the leaders in the market. This also speaks to the level of cooperation present in the industry. For instance, "open systems" encourage dozens of companies to link their success to one or more common forms of technology or service that are offered by leaders in the industry. On the other hand, "closed systems" discourage cooperative links as one company seeks to exploit a distinct product or service feature. The best small-caps will operate in nonproprietary markets with open systems that create opportunities for many forms of cooperative links.

Competitive Density

Emerging fast-growth industries typically have low barriers to entry and are therefore constantly spawning new ventures trying to gain a foothold among the more established firms. The best case scenario for the small-cap investor is an industry with "optimal" competition. If the competitive landscape is overcrowded with too many entrants, then it could be very difficult (if not impossible) to find long-term success. On the other hand, if the industry offers no competition, it could hurt the potential for compatibility and the scope of applications in the market. Certainly, the ideal situation is to find a radically innovative firm and get in on the ground floor before there is any competition. But the best growth industries are the ones that have plenty of opportunity for a consistent stream of new entrants to emerge. Lots of competition is good for the industry in the long run, because it keeps open the prospects for newly launched ventures to stake a claim in the various segments and niches in the market.

A "Classic" Perspective

Princeton Professor Burton Malkiel's essential investment work, A Random Walk Down Wall Street, has been a true classic guide to stock and portfolio management for more than 25 years. With regard to fundamental analysis of the economy, the industry, and the firm, he writes: "Over long periods of time, [professionally managed] mutual fund portfolios have not outperformed randomly selected groups of stocks. While funds may have very good records for certain short-term periods, there is generally no consistency to superior performance. The only dependable relationship is the tendency for funds assuming greater risks to earn, on average, a larger long-run rate of return.'" In light of this pervading commentary, small-cap investors should recognize that a greater propensity for risk assumption is a key component of buying small-cap stocks. As such, the entrepreneurial perspective for managing such risk over the long-term can make small-cap investing very rewarding indeed.

Resources and Referrals

The small-cap investor needs to develop a consistent strategy for locating newly emerging industries and business trends. There are several ways to do this. The first step is to subscribe to a weekly business news magazine and consistently read about the new ideas that are currently in the early development stages. The goal is to get into a regular pattern of watching trends in new products, services, and the industries that are affected by such innovations. A second step is to periodically review selected company analysis reports and summaries presented by the leading rating agencies, such as *Moody's Industrial Manual, Standard & Poor's Stock Guide,* and *Value Line.* Granted, this is public information that is available to all investors, but over the course of just 12 to 18 months of consistent reading and review, a small-cap investor can really begin to develop an excellent perspective as to which industries are moving forward and which are not. A third approach involves attending significant industry trade shows throughout the year. Walking the floor of a large convention center for two days can put the small-cap investor face-to-face with a good deal of owner-entrepreneurs who are very interested in discussing their firm's prospects within the industry. Picking up industry literature, hearing presentations about current and expected product-service trends, and seeing firsthand the range of firms actively involved in product development and partnerships can all hone an overall perspective of an industry's growth potential.

There are numerous economic reference periodicals that directly address specific industry issues. Following is a sample of some public reference industry resources:

1. Government reports (e.g., *The Bulletin of the Federal Reserve Bank of Cleveland*)

2. Industry trade journals (e.g., *META group Client/Server Tools Bulletin*)

3. Industry "white papers" (these are summaries of the discussions, planning, and expectations for the future of an industry usually composed by the leading firms in the industry that are helping to set the research and sales agenda for the next several years)

4. Specialty publication books and summaries (there are numerous books that come out each year profiling industries and providing commentary on where the next significant trends will come from)[5,6]

5. Academic and research Websites (many colleges and universities, as well as scientific and manufacturing research centers, sponsor Internet sites that serve as central locations for discussions and shared ideas on emerging product and service innovations)[7,8]

6. Professional associations (many business and metropolitan areas have private groups that sponsor regular monthly or quarterly seminars and dinners focused on emerging industries and new venture development)[9]

7. Government agencies (there are many federal organizations that actively promote private enterprise development)[10]

However, the primary caveat that must be clearly understood is that many of these resources are (by definition) outdated by the time they come to press or show up on a Website. Business changes very fast, and "hot" trends can fizzle out without much advanced notice. Small-cap investors cannot consult these resources only sporadically. Staying plugged into these kinds of resources must be part of a disciplined program of regular weekly, monthly, quarterly, and semiannual review and analysis. Remember, an idea that looked promising six months ago can lose its luster based on subtle shifts in technologies and consumer behavior. And ideas that were regarded as "highly questionable," can quickly turn around and gain a major following in the market. That is what makes small-cap investing risky and exciting and, for some, highly rewarding as well.

Notes

1. Greenwald, John, 1998. "Crazy Stock Ride," *Time*, July 20, pp. 42–43.

2. Ibid.

3. Newton, David, 1996. "A Qualitative Perspective Model for the Valuation of Knowledge-Based Assets," in C.K. Bart (ed.), *Managing Intellectual Capital and Innovation* (Hamilton, Ontario, Canada: The Innovation Research Centre), pp. 33–43.

4. Malkiel, Burton, 1990. *A Random Walk Down Wall Street* (New York: W.W. Norton), p. 170.

5. Malonis, Jane A. and Holly M. Seldon, 1998. *Encyclopedia of Emerging Industries* (New York: Gale Publishing).

6. Jasinkowski, Jerry, 1998. *The Rising Tide: The Leading Minds of Business and Economics Chart a Course Toward Higher Growth and Prosperity* (New York: Wiley)

7. *The Innovation Management Network*: www.aom.pace.edu/tim/

8. The Management of Intellectual Capital-MINT: http://mint.mcmaster.ca/

9. The Massachusetts Institute of Technology Enterprise Forum (about two dozen local chapters throughout the United States).

10. The U.S. Small Business Administration and its three dozen sponsored Small Business Development Centers, located throughout the United States.

Identifying Innovative Small-Cap Firms

Whenever a small-cap fund manager is interviewed about how individual stocks are actually selected, the conversation generally focuses on a "system" or special (and probably proprietary) in-house methodology used to differentiate the good stocks from the bad ones. Do managers have secret crystal balls that reveal the next crop of high-growth small-cap stocks? Probably not. Instead they most likely have an expert system that screens companies across many different factors to arrive at a profile with the characteristics that are consistent with the portfolio manager's personal bias about what makes a great small-cap investment. Having developed a systematic approach to screening emerging industries, and innovative products and services, the next step for the small-cap investor is to examine individual firms and identify those that are extremely well positioned to take advantage of newly introduced technologies and processes. These companies will be either those that are involved in driving an emerging industry, those that are strong in a tangent industry and poised to make the crossover to the emerging market, or those that are making product and service innovations into existing markets. The small-cap investor must categorize a prospective pool of public firms across these three levels of growth potential. "Clearly, there can be no single foolproof formula for fresh thought and action that will be applicable to every field of endeavor. But there are recurring themes . . . [and]

discernible attitudes that have given organizations a distinct competitive edge when consciously nurtured and actively practiced on all levels."[1]

This chapter discusses the particular characteristics of each grouping and then provides an objective rating scale by which to rank companies from "preferred" through "wait-and-see" status. Again, the emphasis is placed on evaluation, research, and analysis using public information. It is assumed that the stock market is at least weak-form efficient (as defined in Chapter 4), but perhaps not entirely semistrong-form efficient, and that extraordinary stock returns are available to investors who do their homework, understand the rationale behind a small-cap strategy, and construct portfolios with clear performance objectives based upon expected risk and return.

Small-Cap Screen "System"
The truly effective small-cap strategy is far more complex than simply buying into a few firms that have recently gone public. Investors must commit to an ongoing process of screening, selection, and portfolio management. Small-cap investing is not a one-time exercise that searches for a few good companies and then bets the house, the car, and the children, on their necessary growth and success. In fact, betting should never be a component of the small-cap investment process. If placing wagers with the hope of quick profits are the main focus of the funds, then Hollywood Park Racetrack or a Las Vegas casino can both provide plenty of thrills with a chance for a big payoff. But small-cap investing is a systematic discipline that requires prudent selection, patience amid short-term volatility, and an entrepreneurial perspective for long-term appreciation in value.

Three Basic Firm Types

This author proposes that, categorically, there are really only three basic types of small-cap firms from which to consider the investment decision: (a) the "preferred" small-cap company, (b) the "prospective" small-cap company, or (c) the "postponed" small-cap company. These represent the final summary groupings of an in-depth screening analysis designed to identify and subsequently rank the firms with the best potential for exceptional growth over the long term. Certainly, these three groupings are not the only classifications for common stocks under review. The eight screening factors discussed next, likewise, do not constitute an industrywide consensus as to what delineates the best stocks from the worst. However, in the overall context, these categories and varied screening factors are aimed at establishing relative levels of investment interest among typical small-cap investors. Together these constructs provide a thorough process by which small-cap candidates can be systematically previewed prior to the selection of the portfolio's holdings.

Preferred Companies

Small-cap companies with the highest ranking from the pool of stocks under consideration can be described as *preferred*. These are the first shares purchased for the portfolio and represent the best prospects for growth. This does not necessarily mean that each company scored high on every one of the eight screening factors. It simply means that these firms had the highest overall scores, taking into consideration the impact of all the factors. Preferred companies may actually have medium-to-low scores in half the areas but exceptionally high scores on a few factors deemed most important by the portfolio manager. For example, a firm that does not have the best financial scores may have extremely dominant market position and links with several "key" business partners in the industry for joint work that has tremendous potential for long-term growth. The small-cap investor might allow these dominant factors to offset some questionable areas and thus provide a high overall rank for the firm.

Prospect Companies

Small-cap firms with the middle rankings from among the pool of stocks being considered can be described as a *prospect*. These are the shares that *might* be purchased for the portfolio within the next six months or so. The portfolio manager believes these stocks represent average prospects for growth. This does not necessarily mean that each company scored average on every one of the eight screening factors. It simply means that these firms had average overall scores, taking into consideration the impact of all the factors. Generally, these kinds of companies require some additional information, a few more phone calls, and perhaps some extra research on their profile. These firms are poised to be added to the portfolio once the new information is available and their relative ranking improves.

They may have one high score on a given factor, but that is offset by a very low score in another factor. If the overall profile of the firm is neither strong nor weak, the company could be a great stock to buy now in anticipation of something turning around in the next year. On the other hand, it might be prudent to wait and see before purchasing shares. These companies will be watched very closely in the near-term for signals of increased profit expectations.

Postponed Companies

Small-cap firms with the lowest rankings from among the pool of stocks being reviewed can be described as *postponed*. These are the shares that will be dropped from consideration for the portfolio because they represent minimal prospects for growth. Remember, just because a publicly traded company has small market capitalization, that does not mean it is automatically poised for rapid growth. Many small companies remain in an isolated niche and never expand their products and services to other markets. These are postponed because only the prospect stocks will merit constant monitoring to see if anything appears ready to change that would reclassify them as preferred firms. This does not necessarily mean that each postponed company scored low on every one of the eight screening factors. It simply means that these stocks had low overall scores. Typically, these kinds of companies are put on the shelf for now and replaced by other prospective firms. And some of these can become prospect companies in the future as their situation changes. These firms will not be considered for the portfolio for quite a while, unless some new information becomes available and their relative ranking improves dramatically.

Screen Factors

The three firm types can be systematically delineated using eight factors that are exhibited by all firms under consideration for inclusion in a small-cap portfolio strategy. Although there is no entirely objective means to assess each company relative to these factors, the small-cap investor can use a system like this to screen important information about various firms in order to arrive at a relative rank order of which stocks have better growth potential than others. Virtually all small-cap fund managers use a rating sequence process of some sort. The vast majority of these selection programs are obviously proprietary in design, and the only way to know if the model works is to measure the performance of the fund over a minimum period of four-to-five years. But any small-cap investor can effectively implement a screening process that highlights good purchases to make now, and prospective companies to watch closely in the near term.

The screening process presented in this book is composed of eight factors that are selected from among perhaps dozens of potential measures available in the contemporary market. It is very important to note that certain criteria that are deemed "insightful" by one small-cap portfolio manager, may be altogether disregarded by another manager. Or the relative value of a measure used by one individual may not meet the standards established by a different person. Selection criteria are a function of personal biases as to what is considered pertinent and insightful regarding the task of uncovering hidden value in certain companies. Small-cap stock selection reflects a personal bias. In Chapter 7, samples of small-cap funds and managers' selections will be presented as they relate to this screening process. Then in Chapter 10, the portfolio management used by various small-cap fund managers will be examined as well. Tried and tested growth signals are difficult to pinpoint. The following are eight factors recommended for screening small-cap stocks:

1. Level of contribution to the industry

2. Current competitive positioning in the industry

3. Current market share in the industry

4. Management team

5. Pending and potential future partnerships

6. Degree of government regulation involved

7. Marketing range and reach of the products or services

8. Financial structure of the firm

Small-cap investors can use these eight factors to effectively evaluate any company. Typically, the process requires a good deal of due diligence, and discriminating decisions at each stage, as to whether a firm displays the kind of profile consistent with the overall risk and return objective of the small-cap investor. Figure 5–1 summarizes how these eight

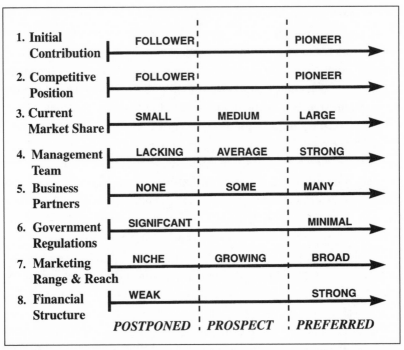

FIGURE 5–1   Screen Factors Used to Classify Small-Cap Companies

factors can be individually scaled and interpreted to most closely represent one of the three basic firm types. The following sections discuss the specific details of each factor and how to interpret the decision process at each stage. Remember that many of the best factors used in the industry are not quantitative, but qualitative. There are often no specific ways to apply the criteria. The small-cap investor must provide an informed rationale and clear portfolio objectives when using screen factors. After each factor is reviewed, a complete flowchart is presented that shows how to use all the factors together to place companies in one of the categories. The chapter concludes with several case examples of small-cap firms sorted by category using this system.

Initial Contribution

The first variable measures the degree to which the company has contributed to the emerging market opportunity. Essentially it asks: Did this firm originally introduce this technology or process to the industry? In response to that question, a firm can either be a pioneer or a follower at the first stage of market contribution. Pioneers bring a new process or technology to the market and exploit this innovation to gain a strong presence right at the outset of the emerging business concept. Followers, on the other hand, jump into the market right behind the pioneer and either produce a copy of the initial innovation or make small incremental improvements to a few select features in the original product offering.

Typically, small-cap firms identified as pioneers have overall scores among the eight screen factors that designate them as preferred investment choices. However, pioneering companies are not the only small-caps worthy of serious investment consideration. Many follower firms at the early stages of market development will also provide excellent opportunities as preferred small-cap investments. On the other hand, sometimes firms that are followers may only be prospects because they have not yet generated a strong enough impact with their market entry. And in many circumstances, a follower can be postponed from current investment consideration. This is often the case when investors believe that an initially fast-growth small-cap company lacks the technological proficiency, production capability, and/or intellectual capital that are necessary to maintain the follower position in the emerging competitive market. Without the right resources and talent, the firm might be unable to press ahead with continued developments and major contributions to the future direction of the industry.

Competitive Position

The previous factor dealt with the initial level of contribution when the new idea was being introduced. This second factor deals with where the firm is today in the present structure of the industry. As was the case with initial contribution, there are arguably only two places a company can be. Either they are still a pioneer, providing product and/or service leadership to the marketplace or they are a follower, involved in emulating and trying to refine the leader's offerings. The firm that continues to pioneer advances in technology and product-service developments is obviously a relatively stronger investment candidate when compared to a company that is following in the present market position. At this point it is worth noting that there are now four possible configurations of these first two screen factors. Figure 5–2 shows these different combinations.

Notice that in the "current position" the company that was initially a pioneer when the emerging industry was being introduced is now following behind a new market leader. This is a "bypassed" firm. The company that was initially a follower at industry inception has now moved into a leadership position. This describes an "overtaker" firm. This small-cap company has aggressively pursued the leadership position with significant commitments to the talent and resources necessary to challenge for a leadership role in the industry. The "trailer" company in the lower right might have aggressively jumped into the market right after the leaders were starting to gain some momentum but it has remained a follower up to the present. Companies like this never secure a distinct competitive advantage and are generally content to borrow ideas and technologies once they have been thoroughly tested by the leaders in the industry. The upper left quadrant describes the company that pioneered the new technology and ideas at the earliest stage of market development and has maintained that position right up to the present time. This is a true "vanguard" firm, always at the forefront, pressing forward, leading the way for everyone else in the industry. These companies possess the resources, talent, and entrepreneurial vision to constantly push the industry further along through

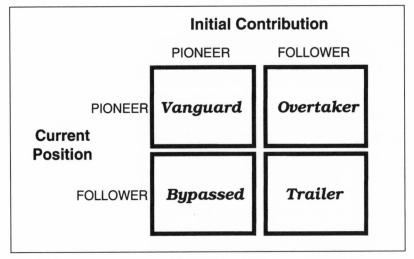

FIGURE 5–2   Competitive Positions in an Emerging Industry

creative ideas and innovative solutions to customer wants and needs. The preferred small-cap stocks are typically vanguard or overtaker companies. Prospects are many times characterized as bypassed firms, although many bypassed stocks could also be viewed as postponed from any near-term investment considerations. Trailer companies are many times postponed from investment consideration, and yet a few may be thought of as having great potential and might qualify as prospects with certain portfolio managers.

Current Market Share

This third factor may initially sound redundant when compared to the previous factor of current competitive position. However, there can be a huge difference between the types of product and service innovations a company brings to the market and the ultimate level of market share that firm secures among customers. Many small-cap companies were pioneering innovators who saw their initially strong market share eroded over time by wave upon wave of new entrants. Others who were followers actually gained on the initial industry leaders. For example, an overtaker firm might have taken over the leadership role from another company in the industry, but they may not yet have turned their newfound fame into a strong market share. Or a bypassed firm might hold onto the number-one sales position in the market, even though other companies have more advanced product and service features. It could also be that a trailer firm has always enjoyed a strong market share presence as a result of exceptional promotions and advertising, as well as widespread distribution and top-of-the-line customer service. Although they have never been an innovator, they are extremely effective at selling and supporting their product or service offerings in the marketplace. It is worth noting that vanguard firms may not always be guaranteed the top slot in market share. Granted, it is highly probable that a pioneer firm with consistent leadership will enjoy a strong sales position. But, sometimes the great "idea people" don't do a very good job of making the transition to a strong commercial application that translates into leading the industry in sales. Typically, market share will be classified as either "large" (preferred and some prospect firms), "medium" (most prospects and a few preferred companies), or "small" (most postponed and some prospect firms).

Management Team

The fourth factor, the management team, is perhaps one of the most crucial components to delineate a firm with strong investment from one with
only moderate potential. The small-cap investor must realize that buying
stock in a firm is in many ways a proxy vote of confidence in the founding
entrepreneur-owner and senior executives. This "team" is responsible for
the strategic direction of the company, the research and product development agenda, the company's competitive position in the marketplace, and
the ultimate profitability and financial success. Due diligence should ask
questions about the personal business philosophy of senior managers. There
should be a demonstrated track record of prior successes in all areas of
marketing, operations, finance, human resources, and innovation development as well as in the ability to forge key strategic partnerships. They
should have clear skills that match their respective area of responsibility
within the firm. Someone with a production and operations background
should not be heading the marketing effort. A human resources and labor
résumé is probably not a good match to oversee the company's accounting and finances. And each key decision maker should have a solid background in *true* senior-level policy formulation and implementation. A
person with an MBA in finance and 10 years experience managing trust
accounts at a regional bank might not really be qualified to negotiate million dollar leasing deals and produce sophisticated cash-flow analysis for
a manufacturing company. Their résumés should have specific descriptions of how they orchestrated new ideas and innovation in other similar
ventures. They should also possess a high level (BA, BS, or MBA) of
formal management training. This does not mean that every manager with
a business degree is worthy of investment backing, but taken in the context of the overall ranking of the management team, the small-cap investor
should include formal education as part of the individual background check.

Small-cap investors must also find out the exact percentage of common stock ownership held by each senior executive. If they are not heavily
invested in the company, there should be doubts about their vested interest
in the long-term prospects of the firm. The founder may have given up a
block of stock to senior executives prior to going public, and another large
proportion at the IPO, but the owner-entrepreneur should still own a solid
stake in the business. It is also important to delineate how much stock has
actually been purchased by senior executives and how much has been re-

ceived over the years as compensation and performance bonuses. The management team should have a demonstrated track record of "holding" the company stock, rather than a history of slowly selling it off year-by-year, or even worse, a pattern of selling off and buying in again on a regular basis. And finally, the overall character of these managers should reflect a well-organized, diversely skilled, and complementary team, with shared responsibilities united under a common vision. Small-cap investors might want to avoid companies in which the founder-owner-entrepreneur does everything or companies that merely have the appearance of a management team. The individual men and women that run the company will be making decisions that directly affect the growth prospects of the small-cap investor's stock portfolio. Their level of competence is a crucial factor in the overall screening process.

The Management Team Is Crucial

Bernice Behar is a senior vice-president and portfolio team leader for the small-cap portfolio: The John Hancock Emerging Growth Fund. She states, "Dr. Newton correctly underscores management capability as one of the critical variables in identifying what will be a successful small-cap company. Beyond the founding leader's 'vision,' his or her ability to attract and retain quality people is at the heart of building tomorrow's big-cap company. We have found that the most successful [small-cap] companies are those that recognize the need to build management depth early on in anticipation of future growth. When we interview a company founder or CEO, we focus on where he or she spends their time and energy."

Current and Potential Partners

The fifth factor describes the strategic business alliances and joint ventures that are already in place for the small-cap firm. Whenever a smaller firm is able to secure strong links with midsized and larger suppliers and distributors who are well established in the industry and related markets, it further strengthens the long-term viability of the small-cap company's revenue (and earnings) stream. The small-cap investor is looking for businesses that have secured joint ventures and strategic marketing partnerships for the intermediate and long term. When smaller companies agree to share technology, jointly advertise their specialty products with a large company's full line of products and services, or build component parts for large firms or sign long-term contracts to distribute for bigger companies, their overall presence in the market is strengthened. Isolated small-cap companies are much less desirable for inclusion in portfolio because the risk of business failure increases dramatically when there are few or no direct links with strategic partners. Now, that does not mean that a stand-alone firm cannot be, overall, a great prospect or even a preferred company. But a conspicuous lack of business alliances will detract from a small-cap stock's investment potential. And in the same way, success is not guaranteed to a small-cap firm just because there are several layers of joint ventures in place. This factor must be viewed in light of potential partners, and the overall profile of the firm. The company's nonsystematic risk can be tremendously decreased when there are strong ties with a wide range of related businesses in place. Risk reduction at this level can clearly separate preferred small-caps from prospects and postponed stocks.

The small-cap investor must also examine the partnership deals and joint ventures that *might be*, or already are, "in the works" with other companies. A small-cap firm might have no existing links with strategic business partners, but it is poised to create a joint research endeavor to manufacture related support products with a 20-year-old firm that has a long-standing reputation for high quality, as well as a huge customer base. This pending deal could be the difference between a firm being classified as a prospect stock versus a preferred small-cap firm. In another instance, a firm might have several smaller, regional partnerships in place, but it is preparing to move to a national scope of operations with a foreign partner. Again, this potential arrangement could make the stock a great preferred investment for the small-cap portfolio.

Government Regulation

The sixth factor looks at the degree of both the existing and possible future government regulation associated with the product or service offerings from the small-cap firm. Long-term product-testing cycles, hearings before regulatory agencies, and screening for potential health or environmental risks can each significantly slow the company's response time in the market. If an emerging business will have significant costs and time constraints imposed by various federal, state, and/or local regulatory agencies, these will contribute increased risks to the feasibility of the business, as well as the long-term viability in the market. However, if there are very few, or no, legal issues pertaining to the company's core operations, this can either reduce or eliminate certain risks that could affect growth prospects. Typically, a small-cap firm is either faced with minimal government regulations (preferred and prospects) or extensive regulations because of the industry (postponed firms).

Marketing Range and Reach

The seventh factor deals with marketing and is really composed of two distinct measures that are rarely calculated as part of normal monthly business summaries. A small-cap company's marketing *range* and *reach* are crucial indicators that can pinpoint the source and potential of future growth, and how it will most likely occur. *Marketing range* describes the breadth of a firm's sales across the various segments that comprise the market. For example, an industry may have seven segments that range from smaller specialty wholesalers, through midsized distributors, on up to large national retailers. One-quarter of industry sales may be concentrated among the 10 nationally ranked volume buyers at one end of the spectrum, while the remaining 75 percent of sales are divided between the dozens of customers spread across the other six segments of the continuum.

Marketing reach measures how far the firm's products and services have penetrated each individual segment of the range. For instance, the seven segments just described each contain a pool of potential buyers. Some are long established, others are up-and-coming, and a few might be new entrants. A company's reach describes the percentage of buyers in each segment that order products and services. Sales might come from just 15 percent of the available customers in a given segment, or from more than 90 percent of the companies.

Figure 5–3 shows the relationship between the small-cap company's marketing range and marketing reach. Small-cap investors can estimate how widely dispersed the firm's revenues are across the range of buyers in the market, and then forecast the concentration of sales (the reach) in each segment. In this example, the firm's range only covers three of the five major market segments. The company's reach extends well into the buyers from market segment A, but only slightly into segments D and E. A typical analysis may show five or six segments, and each of these will

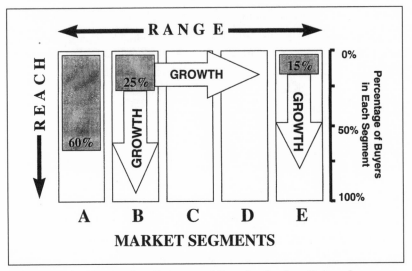

FIGURE 5–3   Marketing Range and Reach of a Small-Cap Company

have a rank order (low to high) of dozens (or more) buyers in each segment. This provides an initial overview of the range across the entire market, and the reach within each segment. Many small-cap companies are not represented in some segments. There could be a distinct combination of either a wide or narrow "core" range, with a deep or shallow core reach.

The best possible growth signal is when sales represent a wide range of segments with only a few core buyers in each (less than, say, 25 percent customer reach). This offers growth potential for further penetration into existing market segments. Or perhaps the firm has good penetration in one segment (around 60 percent or more reach) but limited (or no) range. This offers growth potential to move across the range into new segments from a strong foothold in another segment. A poor signal is when sales come from just one segment (no range) and only a few small buyers in that area (no reach). The best small-cap firms have plans to target potential buyers in other segments (to widen the range) or untapped buyers within an existing segment (to deepen the reach). The range and reach for small-cap firms are generally categorized as either "niche-only" (postponed), "growing" (good prospects that might even be worth investing in at present), or "broad" in terms of the scope of market impact (preferred firms). The small-cap investor must recognize that some companies have better positions in the competitive market, with products and services that are innovative, well-regarded by buyers, and widely recognized in several tiers of the various customer bases.

Range and Reach Really Matter
John Hancock fund manager Bernice Behar comments, "Dr. Newton has identified in a compelling manner the notion of 'range and reach.' The extent to which a product or service may be adopted across industries is certainly a factor in determining the long-term growth profile of a company. Further understanding the penetration potential that a company has within an industry sector lends additional confidence in the durability of that growth."

Financial Structure

The eighth factor is a very significant matter for the small-cap investor. The company's balance sheet and income statement must meet certain measures of performance with regard to efficiency, profitability, and financial positioning. Pro forma financial reports dealing with working capital, cash flow, capital budgeting acquisitions, and projected returns on assets and equity must demonstrate the necessary capabilities to support the firm in the market. There must also be a clear financial plan to fund the future growth of the company. Because the financial structure is so multifaceted, it will be dealt with in detail in the following chapter. At this point it is important to state that a strong balance sheet and income statement will typically help to classify a small-cap company as a preferred investment. Troubles with debt, earnings, sales, inventory management, cash-flow cycles, or a lack of sustainable profitability will certainly lower the overall screen scoring and strongly impact the classification of the firm.

The Screening Process

In the next section, several firms are systematically examined using the three types of screened companies, as well as each of the eight screening factors. Refer back to Figure 5–1 of an outline of the general configuration of the screening process for small-cap stocks. The eight factors are arranged on the left side and each area is scored from left to right. Generally speaking, a postponed firm has a profile that is overly concentrated in the segment to the far left. A prospect stock has a profile characterized by the center area. Preferred companies have their scores leaning heavily to the far right side of the scoring system. When performing a small-cap profile, a company does not have to have every area scored in the same distinct category in order to be ranked as one of the three types. This is a qualitative system. There is no distinct method to use that will yield exacting classifications. For example, one firm may have several factors scored far to the right, with one or two in the middle and the left, and yet still be classified as a preferred small-cap company. Another firm may have many factors scored in the middle, with a few leaning to the left, and be considered a postponed investment. The small-cap investor is looking to differentiate the pool of potential stocks in a manner that is consistent and based on as clear a rationale as possible. Preferred companies will be purchased and placed in the current portfolio strategy. Prospect firms will be further researched and watched very closely to see if anything changes in the profile mix. A select group of these can actually be purchased now in anticipation of an upcoming change in the industry that would make this company a preferred small-cap. The stocks designated postponed are placed on the back burner, so to speak. They will be revisited maybe once or twice in the next six-to-nine months, but there are significant market, financial, and/or operations issues that must be resolved before they will be considered prospects that merit a constant and close watch by the portfolio manager.

Preferred Company Sample Profile

Figure 5–4 summarizes the profile of a typical small-cap preferred company. Notice that, although the firm was a follower in initial contribution, it is now at the forefront of the industry's technology innovations with medium market share (good room for sales growth). The business has some existing partnerships in place and more to follow in the projected near term. There is also little current or expected negative impact from government regulations. The firm's marketing range is still not as wide as it could be, and there remains excellent opportunity to deepen its reach into several existing market segments (also points to plenty of room for sales growth). Overall, the firm has a sound financial structure. This small-

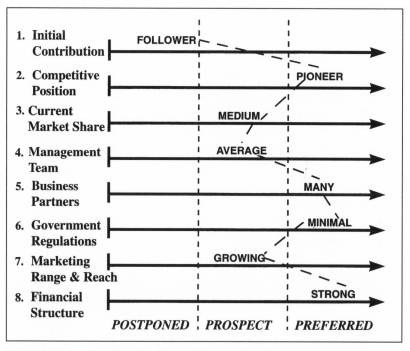

FIGURE 5–4 Profile of a Typical Small-Cap Preferred Company

cap profile is very positive and points to strong potential for growth in the next few years.

Prospect Company Sample Profile

Figure 5–5 summarizes the profile of a typical small-cap prospect company. Notice that the firm was one of the original pioneers in terms of the initial contribution of a technology or process application (a product or service), but the company has now been bypassed by other firms who are much better positioned to lead the industry's technology innovations. The company has a medium-sized market share (there is definitely some room for sales growth), but it has no current business partnerships in place and just a few small deals that are either pending or not very significant for the projected near term. There is also a reasonable potential that certain newly sanctioned state laws will require the company's product(s) to meet a variety of safety standards that could slow down production times, add to

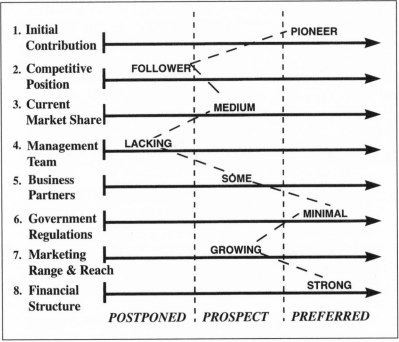

FIGURE 5–5 Profile of a Typical Small-Cap Prospect Company

materials and labor costs, and shrink profits dramatically. The firm's marketing range could be wider, as there are only a few industry segments represented among the customer base. And there are also excellent opportunities for the company to deepen its reach into several existing and new market segments. Finally, the firm has a reasonably sound financial structure. This small-cap profile has some positive points as well as negative issues that make it a prospective stock to watch carefully over the next few years.

Postponed Company Sample Profile

Figure 5–6 summarizes the profile of a typical small-cap "Postponed" company. Notice that the firm was a follower in initial contribution, and it remains one of the many followers in the industry's current technology development trends. The company has a small market share and no current or potential business partnerships in place. Some potential for negative impacts exist from regulations at the federal level. The firm's marketing range is not very wide, but that is due to primarily to a narrow niche market. Overall, the firm has a somewhat weak financial structure. This small-cap profile is more negative than positive, so any further review of this small-cap stock will be postponed a few years.

Relative Positions
Screening small-cap firms is not an exact science. The methodology proposed in this book does, however, provide a clear process by which potential investment in certain stocks can be evaluated in a thoughtful and consistent manner. There will always be cases where a true prospect might be inadvertently classified as a postponed company. But these types of categorical miscues will no doubt be based on the lack of accurate information on the part of the small-cap investor. Some would argue that there is no such thing as a purely absolute preferred small-cap profile. And it may be true to some extent that there are only stocks that are "relatively" better choices to invest in versus other companies. But there may be merit to the idea that some firms are inherently excellent choices because of their strengths across various screening factors, because good stock selection is measured not only against the other competing stocks that were under current review.

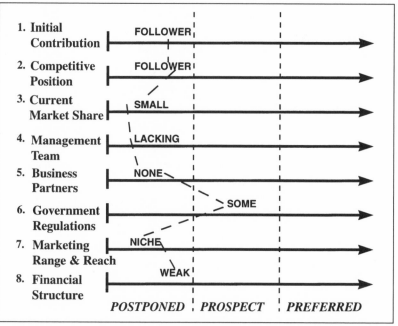

FIGURE 5–6   Profile of a Typical Small-Cap Postponed Company

A strong entrepreneurial perspective will provide an eye toward the future and a vision for emerging venture development. The system will monitor firms as they mature and change over time. Small-cap investors must simply decide when the signals appear promising enough to buy shares for the portfolio.

Conclusion

The most interesting small-cap firms will always demonstrate a tremendous propensity for innovative ideas that translate into tangible, highly successful products and services in the commercial market. Information technology (IT) still depends on "chip size and clock speed,"[2] and innovative firms will continue to press the limits on applications of new ideas and processes across all types of industries. "Knowing how to mesh business and technical planning must replace the old tradition of delegating the administration of computers and telecommunications to technical specialists. Fortunes have been lost, as well as made, on business initiatives that relied on IT."[3] Highly innovative small-cap firms will utilize IT across all aspects of product development, product design, marketing range and reach, as well as distribution channels. Applications will include manufacturing as well as customer service and financial controls. Small-cap investors must commit to those companies that demonstrate an ability to effectively utilize IT to create long-term competitive advantage in the market. This said, the small-cap investor should consider very carefully the fundamental "business" of the firm and the strength (both inherent and comparative) of the company's potential for growth over the long-term. There are no guarantees, but certainly a well-conceived and systematic "process for picking" is better than simply buying small-cap stocks just because they are small or just because they have a nice logo or ticker symbol.

Notes

1.   Diebold, John, 1990. *The Innovators*. (New York: Truman Talley Books), p. 283.

2. McKenney, J., 1995. *Waves of Change* (Boston: Harvard Business School Press), p. 208.

3. Keen, Peter, 1991. *Shaping the Future* (Boston: Harvard Business School Press), p. 15.

Financial Analysis and Small-Cap Firm Profiles

The previous chapter outlined eight factors that can help small-cap investors screen potential companies for portfolio inclusion. Perhaps the most revealing look into a company's operating capabilities comes from a comprehensive financial analysis. This chapter provides an overview of specific financial measures that comprise the eighth and final screen factor for selecting small-cap stocks proposed in Chapter 5. Most, if not all, of the other seven factors tend to be somewhat qualitatively oriented. They require the small-cap investor to make a judgment call as to their status and relative worth in the screening process. On the other hand, financial analysis tends to be more quantitative, using calculations of various numbers from the firm's financial statements. But even the quantitative summaries developed here will require the small-cap investor to make qualitative assessments about what the data are really "saying" about the company. Each individual investor and fund manager will ultimately determine what is critical, what is important, and what can be ignored when it comes to interpreting a wide range of financial measures.

A small-cap investor does not have to be a chartered financial analyst (CFA) to gain valuable insights into the pool of candidate firms by performing a comprehensive financial summary. The following sections describe a select group of financial ratios and measures that are critical in determining the long-term viability of the business venture. Figure 6–1 shows the relative placement of financial analysis in the small-cap invest-

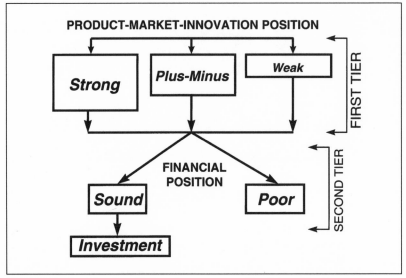

FIGURE 6–1   The Small-Cap Investment Decision-Making Hierarchy

ment decision-making process. Financial analysis must be viewed in the overall context of the other seven factors, and not in isolation, in order to draw a truly comprehensive picture about the firm's strengths and weaknesses. The first tier involves the first seven factors discussed in Chapter 5. The second tier focuses on the results of the balance sheet and income statement commentary. Too many financial analysts place all their trust in balance sheet and income statement calculations alone. But these measures must be seen as complements to the marketing, sales promotion, production and operations, research and development, joint partnerships, and senior management positions of the firm. For many investors, fundamental research begins with the financial statements in a typical "bottom-up approach" to firm analysis. The problem with this tactic is that some companies have strong balance sheets and income statements, yet they lack the industry presence or management capability to truly make a significant and lasting impact in the competitive market. The best approach is to allow the financial analysis to serve as the final confirmation or exclusion *after* the previous seven factors have been reviewed. In this manner, the company's financial position either closes the decision to invest, or it signals that the manager should wait before including the stock in the portfolio holdings.

Having completed a comprehensive financial analysis of the proposed firm, there are six possible scenarios that can result. Figure 6–2 summarizes these different situations. The first-tier line of reasoning involves the commentary on the company's innovative contribution, market position and share, marketing range and reach, partnership arrangements, and any impacts of government regulations. The second tier makes a judgment about the firm's financial positioning. This serves as the final screen, to either confirm the investment, question the current timing of the investment, or exclude the stock from further consideration. A preferred company merits investment. The stock clearly appears to be a strong candidate for growth. A prospect company is a small-cap stock that will be watched very closely in the near term for improvement in either its financial position or other product-market-innovation areas. Companies that are postponed from further tracking and passed over for current investment may be looked at again in a year or so, at a time when significant changes occur in the market or the company's financial position. Notice that the upper left box represents the strongest investment decision (preferred companies) and the lower right box represents the very weakest small-cap candidates (postponed companies). But pay close attention to how the financial analysis serves as a final deciding factor for prospect companies where there is indecision between plus and minus factors in their profile. Poor financials postpone plus-minus firms from any further consideration and

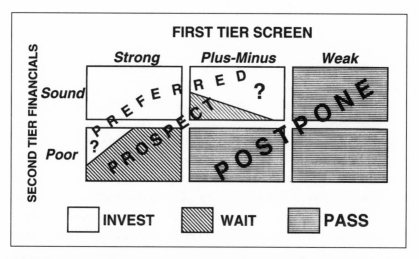

FIGURE 6–2   The Results of the Small-Cap Screening Process

turn strong first-tier companies into prospects to watch closely. Sound financials can either confirm that a plus-minus firm is in fact a good prospect, or they might be just enough to turn a plus-minus firm into a preferred investment. There is certainly a judgment call that has to be made in the case of the upper middle box, but a comprehensive financial analysis should serve as the final screen in the investment decision process.

The Financial Picture

Several steps must be carefully followed in order to put together the entire "picture" of the company's financial strengths and weaknesses. These steps include: (1) a performance ratio analysis, (2) a multiperiod leverage analysis, (3) a cash-flow analysis, and (4) a growth index analysis. The first step involves financial measures derived from the firm's balance sheet and income statement. The second step will then compare specific performance over time. The third step will make adjustments to the accounting data to measure the true cash flow of the firm. The fourth step applies certain tests of the firm's growth potential relative to the underlying financial performance. The small-cap investor can use both the quarterly and annual reports sent to shareholders by the firm, as well as the 10-Q (quarterly) and 10-K (annual) reports that the company must file with the Securities and Exchange Commission.

Balance Sheet Basics

There are numerous ways to approach a small-cap company's balance sheet. Several key pieces of information can be pulled from a careful analysis of the basic accounting categories of assets, liabilities, and owner's equity. But first, rethink what these three categories really mean to the company. Assets are simply everything that firms have to work with in the execution of daily operations. Current assets are things like cash in the bank and short-term securities for transactions, receivables to be collected, materials in process of manufacturing or assembly, and inventory waiting to be sold. Fixed assets are buildings, trucks, licenses, patents, contracts, and equipment to make business happen each day. And everything they have, they either owe money on (short-term and long-term liabilities), or own outright (equity). So the best way to think about firm accounting is that everything companies have equals what they owe plus what they own (assets = liabilities + equity). Small-cap investors need to have preset guidelines about how far in debt a company should be before that debt starts to jeopardize steady cash flow and profitability. Do not start the financial analysis by examining the balance sheet line item by line item. Instead, start with the big picture of what the company has to work with (the assets). Are the assets a good mix that is appropriate for the production and marketing needs in the competitive environment? Did the owners make good choices in what to acquire and employ in the daily business operations? Do they have the "right stuff," the necessary capabilities to maintain a strong presence relative to customers and the competition? Assets are like an investment portfolio. Senior management has either made good choices or bad choices in setting the company up for doing business. Each of the following sections, which discuss ways to assess how financially sound a firm is, concludes with a concise summary statement of the objective for each measure.

Current-to-Fixed Ratio

It is essential to figure out the mix between current assets and fixed assets. If a company is heavy on cash, inventory, and receivables, it might call into question whether senior management has the appropriate commitment to the manufacturing capital base and critical equipment for marketing and operations support. If the firm is light in current assets, it is imperative to know if that is by design or simply because the firm lacks a reliable source of working capital to carry cash-flow requirements during periods of short-term business fluctuations. The objective of the measure: *To gain a summary sketch of the small-cap firm's basic liquidity with respect to short-term asset investment configurations.*

FORMULA

Current-to-Fixed Ratio =
Total Current Assets ÷ Total Fixed Assets

Current, Quick, and Debt Ratios

Next, examine the basic way these assets have been acquired. The current ratio compares all the current assets to all the current liabilities. Different industries have certain guidelines, but typically this should be around 2:1.

The quick ratio is the same but excludes inventories from current assets in the numerator. This should be at least 1:1. Companies with higher ratios (greater than 2:1 and 1:1, respectively) are more liquid in the short-term and can finance increased cash-flow requirements internally. Those that are under 2:1 and 1:1 lack the basic working capital necessary to support the short-term highs and lows of cash flow.

FORMULA

Current Ratio =
Total Current Assets ÷ Total Current Liabilities

FORMULA

Quick Ratio =
(Total Current Assets – Inventory) ÷ Total Current Liabilities

Liquidity is essential to the firm's viability in the market, especially when the industry is growing rapidly, and receipts on new sales and invoices due on inventory are not timed to each other. The debt ratio simply shows what percentage of the assets have liabilities outstanding. Again, some industries require significant plant and equipment financed with loans, and others employ a much smaller fixed asset base, with little or no debt. The most obvious issue is that a large percentage of debt (say, 35 percent or more) requires the firm to make loan installment payments that can greatly diminish (or eliminate) firm profitability. So, low debt (25 percent or less) is good, and no debt is best. The objective of the measure: *To determine the true sufficiency of the small-cap firm's liquidity with regard to short-term and long-term debts and whether interest charges on liabilities pose a threat to operating income.*

FORMULA

Debt Ratio =
Total Debt Outstanding ÷ Total Assets

Inventory Turnover

Small-cap investors should look carefully at how quickly the company's products move through the operations and turn into sales in the market.

Inventory turnover compares the firm's cost of the goods sold (COGS) to the average level of inventory carried throughout the year. It is very simple to understand. Inventory that turns over quickly is better than inventory that is slow moving. Remember, short-term funds tied up in inventory that is not moving will ultimately affect short-term liquidity and the timing of the company's cash flow. The objective of the measure: *To examine how quickly the firm's products move and whether this puts a strain on short-term working capital management.*

FORMULA

Inventory Turnover =
Annual COGS ÷ Average Inventory on Hand

Receivables Turnover

The firm must demonstrate that it can collect outstanding bills in a timely manner. Receivables turnover compares the annual credit sales to the average level of accounts receivable on the books. If the denominator is significantly smaller than the numerator, it shows the company has most credit sales collected. Again, this affects liquidity and cash flow. Firms that can quickly turn the credit they extend to buyers into cash receipts have more liquidity available for growth. And as was the case with inventory turnover, firms with slow receivables turnover have too much cash tied up in their customer accounts. The objective of the measure: *To know how quickly the firm is able to convert sales into cash and whether this also puts a strain on short-term working capital.*

FORMULA

Receivables Turnover =
Annual Credit Sales ÷ Average Receivables on Hand

Asset Turnover

The next key focus should be on the link between the balance sheet and the income statement, namely asset turnover. Compare the firm's sales revenues to the assets configured in the business. Do the current and fixed assets generate a strong flow of sales into the company? Different industries have unique benchmarks, but typically a business should be able to bring in a strong multiple of sales revenues (better than 3:1) on the assets employed in daily operating. It is a direct commentary on the value of the assets in which senior management has invested. If sales are weak compared to the assets assembled, an explanation is needed as to why revenues are not stronger. The objective of the measure: *To determine if management's present configuration of the fixed and current asset investment portfolio generates sufficient sales.*

FORMULA

Asset Turnover =
Annual Sales Revenues ÷ Total Assets

Income Statement Insights

Now that the assets and the level of sales generated on those assets have been examined, the next issue involves what happens to the sales that come into the firm. The most crucial concern for the small-cap investor should be the firm's ability to turn sales into a strong and reliable profit. Think of the income statement as having three tiers. The first tier is where the company turns sales revenues into a gross profit. It all begins here. If the firm has a great product aimed at the right target market, sales should be strong and consistently growing quarter by quarter. After direct labor and materials costs (COGS) of production are subtracted, the firm shows what is called the *gross profit*. The second tier tracks gross profits that are then allocated to fixed costs such as salaries, facilities and rents, various types of insurance, promotional and advertising expenses, license fees, and other overhead expenses not directly related to sales volume. *Operating profit* is what remains after these costs are subtracted from gross profits. The third tier tracks what happens to operating profit as interest and taxes are paid. The result is the "bottom line," or *net profit*. With sound management, sales turn into gross profit at the first tier, into operating profit at the second tier, and into net profit on the third tier.

Gross Profit Margin

The gross profit is shown as a percentage of the sales from which it was generated. Obviously, the larger the gross profit the better. Firms that have gross profit margins of less than 30 percent will find it difficult to manage the second and third tier to a strong net profit unless they can sell a very large volume of products or services. Companies with margins of more than 50 percent have the best prospects for strong profitability. Margins between 30 and 50 percent can go either way, based upon the management's ability to monitor costs effectively. The objective of the measure: *To determine whether labor and materials are well managed relative to the firm's prices on products and services.*

FORMULA

Gross Profit Margin =
Annual Sales Revenues – COGS ÷ Annual Sales Revenues

Operating Profit Margin

The ratio of operating profit (earnings before interest and taxes, or EBIT) compared to sales is a crucial insight into how operations are budgeted and managed by the firm. The proxy of a small-cap company's ability to manage fixed overhead costs, operating margin, is generally unrelated to gross margin. For instance, many companies with large gross profits cannot keep overhead under control and lose most, if not all, of their first tier profits at the second tier. Other companies act prudently in managing overhead costs and generate a strong operating margin on a relatively low gross margin. A good measure is to compare the operating margin to the gross margin. The closer the ratio is to 1 the better. Think of it as the percentage of gross profits that make it through the second tier into operating profit. As a rule of thumb, the higher the margin, the better for the firm. The objective of the measure: *To see if fixed overhead costs are well-managed relative to the company's sales volume and gross profits.*

Time Interest Earned

Interest payments on outstanding debts are then paid from operating profits. Firms with high debt ratios lose a good deal of their operating profits to debt costs. Time interest earned (TIE) measures the company's operating profits compared to its interest payments. The larger the ratio, the more operating income profit turns into net profit. The objective of the measure: *To find out if interest payments on various short-term and long-term debts place too much pressure on the firm's operating profitability.*

Net Profit Margin

Once gross profits are earned on sales, operating profits are earned after fixed costs, and provisions are made for interest and taxes, the firm reports its net after-tax income. This can also be measured as a profit margin on a percentage of sales basis. Different industries vary, but a well-managed growing company should be able to produce a net margin of between 5 and 10 percent. This net profit also forms the basis for reporting earnings per share to the stockholders in the market. The objective of the measure: *To establish a strong commitment to profitability on the part of senior management, and to see if they possess the necessary capabilities to generate strong profits on the firm's expected future sales volume.*

FORMULA

**Net Profit Margin =
Net After-Tax Earnings ÷ Annual Sales Revenues**

Multiperiod Leverage Analysis

The second step in the financial review involves tracking the firm's recent progress on the three tiers of the previous income statement analyses. Leverage analysis also takes place on three tiers, focusing on sales, operating profits, and net profits over a three- to four-year period of time. The *degree of operating leverage* compares the percentage change in operating profits divided by the percentage change in sales revenues during the selected time period. The larger the ratio the better because it shows management's ability to generate stronger growth in operating profitability from disproportionately smaller sales growth. The *degree of financial leverage* compares the percentage change in net profits divided by the percentage change in operating profits. Again, the larger the ratio the better because it shows management's ability to generate stronger growth in net profitability from disproportionately smaller growth in operating profits. The *degree of combined leverage* compares the percentage change in net profits divided by the percentage change in sales. It is the product of the first two ratios. Table 6–1 shows two different examples of a one-year leverage analysis. Notice that firm A had a strong 24 percent growth in sales that generated less than a 20 percent growth in operating profits and produced only about a 14 percent gain in net profits. The leverage figures are read as follows: Operating profits grew at just 82 percent of the pace of sales, net profits grew at just 73 percent of the pace of operating profits, and net profits only grew at 59 percent of the pace of sales between the two years selected. On the other hand, similarly sized firm B had operating profits grow at almost one and a half times the pace of sales. Its net profit also grew at around one and a half times the pace of operat-

TABLE 6–1   Sample Leverage Analysis for Firms A and B

Firm A	Year 1	Year 2	Change
Sales Revenues	$30.8 M	$38.2 M	+ 24.0%
Operating Profit	$ 5.6 M	$ 6.7 M	+ 19.6%
Net Profit	$ 1.4 M	$ 1.6 M	+ 14.3%

Operating Leverage: 19.6% divided by 24.0% = **0.82**

Financial Leverage: 14.3% divided by 19.6% = **0.73**

Combined Leverage: 14.3% divided by 24.0% = **0.59** = (0.82 × 0.73)

Firm B	Year 1	Year 2	Change
Sales Revenues	$31.4 M	$37.5 M	+ 19.4%
Operating Profit	$ 4.9 M	$ 6.3 M	+ 28.6%
Net Profit	$ 1.2 M	$ 1.7 M	+ 41.7%

Operating Leverage: 28.6% divided by 19.4% = **1.47**

Financial Leverage: 41.7% divided by 28.6% = **1.45**

Combined Leverage: 41.7% divided by 19.4% = **2.15** = (1.47 × 1.45)

ing profits, and overall, net profits grew at more than twice the pace (2.15 times) of sales between the two years. Multiperiod leverage analysis provides insights into the firm's COGS and fixed overhead cost management (sales become gross profits become operating profits), as well as the impact of any newly acquired debt service (operating profits minus interest and taxes yield net profits). The best small-cap firms will have strong leverage measures of greater than 1:1 during periods of rapid sales growth. If costs escalate at either the same pace as sales growth, or even faster, then leverage measures will be less than 1:1.

Cash-Flow Analysis

Although the firm's income statement provides good insights into revenue growth, cost management, and debt service on outstanding liabilities, a somewhat more accurate picture of the company's income and profits comes from cash-flow analysis. Investments into fixed assets like facilities, equipment, machinery, vehicles, licenses, and goodwill provide depreciation write-offs that reduce operating profits for tax purposes. But these deductions are not actually paid out to anyone, so they are added back into the net profits to show the firm's true after-tax cash flow (ATCF). Table 6–2 shows the accounting income statement for firm C for tax purposes on the left, and the true ATCF on the right. Although the firm shows $3.2 million in net after-tax profits (a 10 percent net margin), it actually generated $5.6 million in ATCF on sales (a 17.6 percent true margin). Table 6–3 shows how firm D showed an operating loss of $1.3 million and had no taxes due, but yet it produced $100,000 in positive ATCF.

Cash-flow analysis revealed that firm D could in fact pay its $1 million in interest on debt obligations, even though it had no operating profits from a "tax-accounting perspective." Along these same lines of thinking, analysts will generally want to review the small-cap firm's *cash-flow coverage.*[1] This "coverage" refers to the company's ability to meet its fixed debt obligations and is measured by comparing the firm's operating profit (or EBIT) plus depreciation deductions to the total interest payments due on all outstanding debt. Stronger firms have coverage of four or five times their interest (or higher), while other companies are in a weaker position when they have only two or three times coverage. If a small-cap firm is able to generate only around a 1:1 coverage, its debt service would be considered too large for its cash flow from operations.

TABLE 6–2   Sample Income Statement for Firm C

	Accounting Income	Cash Flow
Sales	$31.8 million	$31.8 million
COGS	– 18.5	– 18.5
Gross profit	13.3	13.3
Overhead	– 8.1	– 8.1
Depreciation	**– 2.4**	**– 2.4**
Operating profit	5.7	5.7
Interest + taxes	– 2.5	– 2.5
Net profit	= $3.2 million	3.2 million
	Depreciation	**+ 2.4**
	ATCF	**$5.6 million**

One of the best and most widely used measures of the small-cap company's cash-flow position is the level of *free-cash flow*. After a firm has paid all its costs of production and operations and the interest on its debt obligations, the combined pretax profit and depreciation deductions are now under the control of the owners or senior management. This cash can either be entirely reinvested back into the firm and show up as *retained earnings* on the equity portion of the balance sheet, or a portion that is not retained can be paid out to common stockholders as a cash dividend. Typically, senior management will only make the dividend decision after first analyzing all possible internal investment projects. These will be ranked in order of profitability based upon the capital budgeting techniques of net present value, internal rate of return, and timing-duration risk of the future cash flows. When the firm has exhausted all possible investment projects, any funds still available are referred to as *free-cash flow*.[2]

Small-cap investors and stock analysts are always very interested in the company's free-cash flow, because it shows the true strength of the firm's earnings capabilities with respect to all the projects and asset investments that must be made in order to stay competitive in the industry. Most analysts will deduct from the company's after-tax cash flow the investment outlays of what they believe to be the "required" projects for a small-cap

TABLE 6–3   Sample Income Statement for Firm D

	Accounting Income	Cash Flow
Sales	$31.8 million	$31.8 million
COGS	– 21.9	– 21.9
Gross Profit	9.9	9.9
Overhead	– 8.8	– 8.8
Depreciation	**– 2.4**	**– 2.4**
Operating Loss	(1.3)	(1.3)
Interest	– 1.0	– 1.0
Net Loss	$(2.3) million	(2.3) million
		Depreciation **+ 2.4**
		ATCF **$100 thousand**

firm to stay on a growth track. The strongest small-cap firms are awash in free-cash flow and liquidity. Not only can they fund the required projects, but they have "extra" funds to do extraordinary research and development, investment projects, or even acquisitions of related businesses. Some companies may have very little or no free-cash flow, but at least they are able to fund investment projects that are required to stay competitive. The weakest companies have negative free-cash flow available. They cannot do even the necessary internal investments to stay competitive, let alone pursue other strategic directions or outside acquisitions. Small-cap investors definitely need to know how to sift through the income statement and balance sheet to determine how well the company generates cash flow from its operations and can position itself for future growth.

Growth-Index Analysis

The final step in the financial review involves determining some form of a growth index for the small-cap firm. Different financial and security analysts at the many regional and national investment banks and institutional investment houses have varying opinions as to what constitutes a reliable

growth index. Empirical evidence must be garnered from primary research into the relative worth of any financial model. The growth index
advocated here measures the relative size of the company's sales, gross
profits, operating profits, and net profits against two key benchmarks. The
first benchmark is the track record of the firm's financial position. This
provides insights into whether the business can support continued growth.
The second benchmark is based on the best firms from the industry that
have larger operations, as well as highly successful companies of similar
size in related manufacturing or service industries. This will compare the
company to those businesses that have already grown to the level targeted
by the small-cap firm and hopefully reveal the kind of asset base and investment capital necessary to achieve that goal.

The four financial measures used to produce the growth index are: (1)
the asset turnover ratio, (2) the gross profit margin, (3) operating profits
on current assets, and (4) the firm's ATCF compared to total assets. Each
of these is tracked over a continuous 12 fiscal quarters, so that as each new
quarter is added to the benchmark, the quarter from the earliest tracking
period is dropped. The growth index will measure the strength of the
firm's profit picture over time, using the quarterly compounded rate of
change in each area and the following index formula:

FORMULA

Growth Index =
[(Operating on Current ÷ Asset Turnover) × (1 − Gross Profit Margin)] ×
(ATCF on Assets)

It is important to note that the index is specifically designed to work
with positive rates of change (growth) in the operating/current, asset turnover, and ATCF/assets ratios. Stable rates of change in the gross margin
are also rewarded (because of the consistency), but highly volatile fluctuations in the gross margin reduce the index.

This index will then be compared to highly successful firms both from
the same industry and in somewhat related industries. Table 6–4 provides
a summary of the 36-month growth index for firm E covering the second
quarter of fiscal 1998 back to the third quarter of fiscal 1995. The company
has experienced only around a 10 percent growth rate in operating profits

generated on current assets, but has shown more than a 15 percent growth rate in sales generated on total assets. This should be closer to a 1:1 ratio. At a ratio of 0.68 it shows that profits from operations on the firm's liquidity position are growing much slower than the sales generated on the overall asset base. The absolute value of the gross margin growth rate should be quite low if the firm has been able to maintain consistent gross profit margins. The complement of this gross growth rate, 0.9535 (1 – 0.0465), is then used to discount the growth rate in ATCF on assets. The resulting figure of 28.17 percent represents the firm's growth index over the last three years. Had the company's asset turnover and operating-on-current ratios been more in line with each other (near 1:1 ratio or higher), the index would be better. On the other hand, had these been closer to 1:1 but the gross margins had changed dramatically up or down, the index would be worse. This index should be compared to two benchmarks: larger firms in the same industry and highly successful similar sized firms in other related industries.

TABLE 6–4   Sample Growth Index for 36-Month Period for Firm E

Fiscal Quarter	Asset Turnover	Gross Margin	Operating on Current	ATCF on Assets
IIQ '98	1.65 times	43.2%	1.13 times	11.4%
IQ '98	1.61	42.6	1.08	10.8%
IVQ '97	1.48	42.7	1.02	10.2%
IIIQ '97	1.51	42.3	0.95	9.3%
IIQ '97	1.42	41.6	0.97	9.8%
IQ '97	1.28	40.6	0.93	10.3%
IVQ '96	1.30	40.8	0.93	9.1%
IIIQ '96	1.18	40.1	0.91	7.2%
IIQ '96	1.22	39.8	0.80	5.0%
IQ '96	1.13	37.5	0.84	4.2%
IVQ '95	1.02	38.1	0.85	3.6%
IIIQ '95	1.05	37.6	0.83	3.3%
Growth rates: 15.35% (Compounded quarterly)		4.65%	10.42%	43.53%

Growth Index: [(.1042 ÷ .1535) × (1 – .0465)] × (.4353) = **28.17%**

For example, a promising small-cap company with a growth index of 17.55 percent might be quite below the three largest firms in the industry at 22.45 percent, 21.37 percent, and 20.92 percent, respectively. The lower index might stem from a highly disproportionate asset turnover and operating-on-current ratio, an erratic gross margin (either positive or negative), or a weak ATCF return on assets employed. Small-cap investors should pay close attention to firms that have a strong track record of large growth index values over time. The focus should be then tied to examining the overall financial picture of these other companies and the kinds of marketing and operations strategies they employ. The index is not to be applied in an overly simplified manner where the small-cap firm tries to quickly change the four financial measures around in order to replicate the index level of the industry leaders. Instead, the relative position of the small-cap firm's growth index serves as a concise summary comparison to alert senior management to potential areas of concern. It might take several quarters (even years) to successfully implement policies that will have a positive effect on the firm's growth index.

As with any financial measure, it is not perfect and must be carefully interpreted when a company has negative input figures. For instance, when a firm has a decreasing rate of change in gross profit margin, the growth index is designed to reward a less volatile change (negative or positive). Consider the example from Table 6–4. If the gross margin had actually *dropped* by an average 4.65 percent, the growth index would remain the same (28.17 percent). This recognizes that any changes in gross margin have been small enough over time that the company is not penalized. If the rate of change in gross margin was very large (negative or positive), that lack of stability would decrease the index. In the case of Table 6–4, if the firm had a negative rate of change in either operating/current, asset turnover, or ATCF/assets, the growth index would also be negative. This serves as a warning signal that an important measure has decreased over time. In the exceptional case where operating/current and asset turnover were both negative, the quotient would be positive and generate a misleading index. However, that is easily remedied because a firm with decreasing rates of change in these important ratios would not be considered for a growth index in the first place.

This measure all by itself is not enough to merit investment into a certain small-cap stock, but it can provide some interesting insights into companies that have a well-configured asset base, steady gross margins, good management of overhead costs, and solid cash flows based on the size of the assets in the business operation.

Considerations

The various measures presented in this chapter help to establish an overall financial picture of the small-cap firm. They are in no way presented as a perfect means of capturing growth potential in an emerging firm, and there are certainly numerous other metrics and proprietary formulas and models that could be used to ascertain specific insights into a company's profitability and asset posture. But well-organized and thoughtful financial analysis should serve as the final screen in determining which companies are preferred investments, which are prospects worth watching, and which should be postponed from further consideration. The best way to utilize financial analysis is in the context of the overall screening process presented in the previous chapter.

Small-cap investors should be very concerned when they come across accounting irregularities in the firm's operations, slow or incomplete reporting of financial statements, and sudden changes in management's tracking of sales, profits, and cost analysis. These are all very obvious signals that the stock is probably not a solid investment candidate. No matter how strong the company looks in terms of screening its products, markets, and innovation, a sound financial picture is the essential final piece of the small-cap investment puzzle. Jim Cramer, a writer for www.thestreet.com advises that "at the first whiff of 'accounting problems,' sell the stock—don't wait . . .when a company gets caught misstating its financial performance, I try to be interested at no price."[3] Strong financials make preferred companies sound investments, and they could even be used to signal a good investment among what might otherwise be considered prospect companies. Poor financials should cause small-cap investors to further question and reconsider what might otherwise appear to be preferred firms. And finally, the financial picture will likely help to confirm a wait-and-see approach on prospects, or could even move them over to the postponed category.

Notes

1. See the complete work of Harrington, Diana R., 1993. *Corporate Financial Analysis*, 4ᵗʰ Edition (Boston: Irwin).

2. See the comprehensive overview in Ross, Westerfield, and Jordan, 1998. *Fundamentals of Corporate Finance* (New York: McGraw-Hill).

3. Cramer, James J., 1998. "Avoid My Mistake," *Time*, July 27, p. 66.

CHAPTER 7

Samples of
Small-Cap Stocks
Companies the Fund Managers Like

I n the last chapter, a comprehensive financial analysis closed out an overview of eight specific components that can serve as common screen factors among small-cap stocks in order to determine which firms exhibit the most promising investment profiles. These financial indicators can serve as excellent reference points in categorizing the best to the worst candidates from the pool of companies being considered for inclusion in a small-cap investment strategy. This chapter will highlight some of the small-cap firms that typify the profiled characteristics discussed in the last four chapters. These are companies that are first and foremost involved in emerging industries, as outlined in Chapter 4. They also possess several, if not all, of the strong characteristics summarized in Chapter 5 that are generally associated with the best of the fast-growth small-cap stocks. And, their financial analysis indicates that these companies are well-positioned in terms of key balance sheet, income statement, cash-flow, and growth-index measures as reviewed in Chapter 6.

The following sections examine specific firms that are preferred by some of the top small-cap fund managers in the United States, and these will be compared to the various selection factors that have already been discussed. The goal is to determine if there are, in fact, any identifiable clusters of similar opinions among various small-cap fund managers regarding the stocks they choose to include in their portfolios. The chapter concludes with some ideas and discussion about the kinds of companies that make excellent small-cap holdings for the next five-to-seven years (1999–2005).

Strong Profiles

Small-cap firms with the strongest profiles are referred to here as *preferred companies*. They are typically very well positioned for growth because a majority of the screen factors are highly favorable. Figure 7–1 serves as a basic checklist for the stocks in question. In the first level of industry analysis, the application scope, product or service orientation, concentration impact, compatibility, and competitive density must together define strong signs that the industry is in fact large, highly innovative, and wide open for growth. The arrows depict how industries either qualify for continued consideration or drop out because of their lack of innovation, growth, and application potential. At the next level of company analysis, the first two screen factors will sort out the very best of the preferred small-caps as pioneering companies that each made a significant *initial*

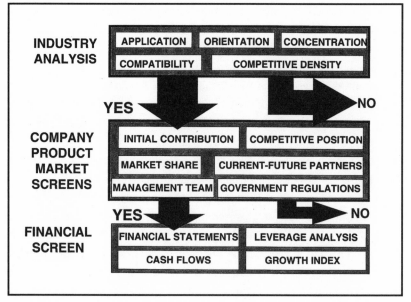

FIGURE 7–1   Checklist for Evaluation of Small-Cap Stocks

contribution to their emerging market and today remain leading innovators in their industries. These firms clearly epitomize the true forerunner. At the third screen factor, they have successfully turned their leadership position into solid sales performance. So the best preferred companies also have some of the highest market share in their industry, and most likely, have always had a strong showing in both volume (units placed) and revenues (the dollar-value of those units sold). Next, these firms have excellent cooperative relationships with other significant players associated with the industry, and have negotiated strong links with suppliers, distributors, and R&D facilitators to support their leadership role in the industry. In addition, they have an eye toward putting into place future partnerships aimed at taking advantage of newly emerging opportunities. The best small-caps use strategic alliances with expert companies to reduce risk exposure and ensure smoother operations. They also have minimal, if any, intrusion risk from government regulations. Small-cap investors continue financial due diligence on those companies with the best preferred and prospect rankings, while postponed companies are dropped from consideration. Following are promising industries and the best preferred firms within each.

Leading Industries and Sample Firms

The Massachusetts Institute of Technology publishes *Technology Review* magazine. MIT claims that its graduates have started some 4000 currently active companies (1998) with combined annual sales of just over $230 billion. Granted, that works out to only $57,000 in average sales per firm. But the top of the list does read like a Who's Who for emerging industries over the last five decades, including companies like 3Com, Analog Devices, Biogen, Bose, DEC, Genentech, Hewlett Packard, Lotus, National Semiconductor, Raytheon, Rockwell, Tandem, Teledyne, and Texas Instruments. A recent perusal of the last several issues of *Technology Review* had articles gushing with growth potential for industries such as biotechnology, chemical engineering, human gene engineering, synthetic materials composite science, computer hardware and software development, and nanoscale mechanical devices for breakthrough medical treatments.[1]

Enduring Perspective

"Just for a moment, think back to where you were ten years ago. There wouldn't be a Web browser for another five years. The federal government had just decided it would allow patents on animals. The Dow closed at 1938.83. And Microsoft Word came on a single diskette. Back then most of us never imagined that 'webmaster' would become a job title . . . satellite dishes would get to be the size of dinner plates . . . 7% of the workforce would become independent contractors . . . somebody would clone a sheep . . . businesses would compete to invest in Russia . . . workers would attend meetings without leaving their desks. Think what life would be like today if you'd known these things were coming and understood their implications."[2]

The editors at *Money World* magazine have identified their own list of fast-growth emerging industries that include direct-link customer selling on the Internet, medical diagnostics, personal leisure watercrafts, educational training, and alternative fuels.[3] The Innovation Research Center sponsored by McMaster University in Hamilton, Ontario, Canada, maintains an interactive Website that hosts regular discussions about emerging industries and breakthrough technologies among a truly international audience of engineers, academics, entrepreneurs, and government agency officials. Recent commentaries have focused on such industries as plasma flat-screen high-density television (HDTV), virtual conferencing, and microwave hydrocarbon detection.[4] Business and technology magazines often have feature stories dealing with fast-rising new industries, such as cyclosporine organ transplant support drugs,[5] interactive television,[6] manned and unmanned subspace stratospheric satellite telecommunications relay,[7] and live audio and video Internet broadcasting.[8] The recent IPO of the Dallas-based firm Broadcast.com (the pioneer in the emerging industry of live Internet broadcasting) experienced a record-setting opening trading day with an offering price of $18, that rose as high as $74, before settling at $62.75, up 248 percent for the day.[9]

A recent cover story expose in *Business Week* discussed the fast-growth industry involved in cutting-edge human tissue-engineering, where numerous recent start-up companies are now turning 20 years of pioneering research into the tangible ability to grow living organs in the laboratory.[10] This new era of "regenerative medicine" is estimated to be an $80 billion industry, spawning dozens of IPOs in the last few years for companies such as ATIS (Advanced Tissue Sciences)—the makers of Dermagraft;

Biomatrix—the makers of Synvisc; Lifecell—the makers of Alloderm; and Organogenesis—the makers of Apligraf. This industry went from exploratory research to marketable products in just the last two years. This newly structured marketplace is joined by a complementary industry that designs and operates virtual human organs on computers in order to "gather information about how organs work that no amount of animal experimentation could provide."[11] Because most organs can be described by relatively simple mathematical equations, these computer-generated organs are complete in every detail, right down to their very cell structure and can be used to screen all kinds of experimental drugs. The potential for long-term growth should merit serious attention from small-cap investors.

Another fascinating industry of the future that is taking shape right now is replacing silicon microchips with "optoelectronic" computers that "combine the speed of light with number crunching power or electrons" using tiny laser and light detectors made from indium phosphide and gallium arsenide.[12] For years these have been cost-prohibitive to design and manufacture. But a pioneering effort, lead by La Jolla, California-based Nanotronics Corporation, is poised to use DNA as a subcellular glue to connect the mutually incompatible indium phosphide and gallium arsenide. Imagine a day in the not-to-distant future when computer users might joke about the days of the 1980s and 1990s when microprocessors *used to be made* out of silicon. Once again, small-cap investors could provide much of the initial market capitalization for firms that might make this industry a prosperous reality.

Every October, *Institutional Investor* magazine ranks the top securities analysts from investment banks around the world based upon (among other criteria) their ability to acquire knowledge of the industry. A quick perusal of the industries represented in the 1997 edition show strong institutional interest in health care, biotechnology, telecommunications, Internet technology, electronics/connectors and components, semiconductor capital equipment, server and enterprise software, wireless equipment and services, and data networking.[13] Special attention is being paid to what are called *technology industries*, such as computers, software, communications, networking, and semiconductors, because growth in these areas is far outpacing the rest of the world economy. Much of this growth is due to better products and services consistently coming to the market at increasingly lower prices. For example, while the semiconductor industry grew from $20 billion in 1980 to $140 billion in 1996, cellular phones powered by these chips went from an initial cost of $3000 and $1.50 per minute to where they are now, costing as little as $20 and just 20 cents per minute.[14]

The Best and Brightest
The very best firms for small-cap investing in these and other emerging industries will be those that exhibit the preferred profile described in Chapter 5. Other prospects will also be worth watching. Remember, these firms may not yet be profitable, which means their current financial picture may not be all that great. But their overwhelming strengths in innovation, product development, and competitive market presence may make them excellent preferred-prospective additions to the small-cap portfolio. Some firms may be borderline between the decision to invest or to wait, simply because their present financial structure has some shortcomings. The screening process is not designed to be an exact science. It can delineate and categorize industries and companies into the best and the worst. But to some degree it will require the subjective intuition of the small-cap investor to sort out the "in-between" companies within the best industries. The three levels of industry and firm-specific analysis summarized in Figure 7–1 cannot guarantee that a preferred company in a top-rated industry will not fail. There might be prospect firms that outperform preferred companies. And some postponed small-cap stocks might turn around very quickly and generate huge gains for investors who had the foresight to buy shares at the initial capitalization and stay put even when financials or product applications did not look decidedly promising early on.

Choice Small-Caps

Within these highly promising industries, small-cap investors are searching diligently for the best preferred profile companies. There is no consensus as to which firms constitute the best investment potential. Of the scores of stocks that continue to surface on the investment schedules of several prominent small-cap funds, there is little (if any) overlap in portfolio holdings. This suggests that small-cap investors may tend to make very individualized stock choices based on highly proprietary selection criteria. For example, this author randomly surveyed 15 small-cap funds (both value- and growth-oriented) as to their respective "top-10 stock holdings." Of the 150 stocks on these 15 lists, there were only three pairs of matches among the funds. These three stocks were Tommy Hilfiger Company, Orion Capital Corporation, and Analogic Corporation.

The differences between these funds were dramatic. One fund was heavy (around 22 percent of its holding) into insurance companies like Orion Capital, Allied Group, and First American Financial, and another had 30 percent in financials, but nearly all the others had either very few financial stocks (around 5 percent or less) or none at all. Technology stocks were well represented as an industry. One fund had 47.7 percent of its holdings in this area, two others had 28.6 percent and 21 percent, but of the remaining 12 funds, none had more than 14.6 percent, and most were at around 10 percent, in the technology category. Healthcare and energy stocks showed up in several portfolios (one had 17 percent in healthcare), but they were typically between 5 and 8 percent of the fund. Consumer products tended to be in most funds as well, with an average allocation of around 8 percent, with two funds in the 20 percent range.

Known Versus Unknown

The greatest risk to the small-cap portfolio is probably not the underlying systematic risk in the broader stock market. The nonsystematic risk that is embedded in firm-specific issues and characteristics will always weigh much more heavily on the small-cap portfolio. No matter how much research and analysis is performed, there will always remain several unknowns associated with the valuation and true potential of an emerging industry and the companies that are making strides to capture the apparent opportunities presented in this marketplace. It would be foolish, and extremely risky, to begin to name specific companies within several emerging industries as being the "best" small-cap investments for the next several years. Certainly this author, like all prudent small-cap investors, has some preferences. But the ability to try to "know" today things that still remain unknown about the future of business is not learned or acquired. Take for example this commentary on the recent explosion of Internet-oriented industries:

> Just a few years ago, analysts were noisily debating the merits of tele-communications versus cable companies. Most hadn't even heard of the Internet. Now the telecom-cable debate seems hopelessly out of date, and such names as America Online, Netscape Communications Corp. and Amazon.com have become veritable blue chips in the brave new world of cyberspace.[15]

Yet many of these rising stars lack the most basic requirements to recommend a stock investment based on a typical financial analysis. With regard to the Internet industry, "Wall Street's conventional assessments—price-earnings ratios and quarterly earnings estimates—sometimes seem irrelevant, even distracting."[16] Mary Meeker, the number-one analyst for tracking Morgan Stanley's list of public Internet stocks, keeps records of IPO dates and price performance, but has dropped the usual earnings (E) column because most of these firms do not have any earnings to report.[17] Neil Weintraut, cofounder of 21st Century Internet Venture Partners, says that "assumptions made just a few years ago—the number of companies that thought they could charge [Internet access] subscriptions fees, for example—are hilariously absurd."[18]

Looking Ahead

It would be very easy to go on and on about the many ways to access the best sources of new information dealing with breakthrough innovations, emerging industries, and the small-cap companies that are pioneering the products and services that will shape our future. The most important concept to take from this chapter is this: *identify reliable sources of industry and company-specific information, and be diligent to stay in touch with the trends and developments on a perpetual basis.* The very best of today's leading industries and small-cap companies were toiling away in virtual obscurity as recently as 5 and 10 years ago. Develop a vision to see *today* the profile characteristics of how similarly positioned contemporary industries will become the leading growth companies of the next 5-to-10 years. Major industrial developments will continue to define the opportunities for small-cap investing. Staying connected to these trends is exciting, and it can be financially rewarding.

The strongest small-cap companies that merit serious investment consideration today will be those that demonstrate clear technological advantages in the emerging industries that have the widest market applications for products and services. Small-cap fund managers know that there are no such things as guarantees when it comes to investing with an eye for the future of new markets. The next round of highly popular and successful products and services are being designed, developed, and test-marketed today. A quick perusal of the "schedule of investments" in the prospectuses of the top two dozen public small-cap funds will provide a window into the personal expectations of various fund managers and research teams around the country.

Should There Be Profits?

My good friend and investment finance colleague, Richard Taylor (who provided the Foreword for this book), is always quick to point out that "It's not too much to ask that the small-cap firm be profitable, is it Dave?" My response is, "Certainly profits are better than losses, Dick, and tangible results are preferable to unsubstantiated hype. But some of the 'best buys' in today's market are not yet profitable, but the prospects are that they will be within a few years." His small-cap fund places a high priority that the prospective company demonstrate profitability with a reasonable likelihood that it is sustainable (and will grow) in the longer term. And yet many of the best small-caps to purchase today may not have profits today, but will remain excellent investments because of their long-term prospects for sales growth and strong future profitability.

Twenty of the leading small-cap mutual funds were reviewed as to their "Top Ten Holdings" and their overall schedule of investments (stocks held in portfolio). Table 7–1 summarizes several dozen small-cap stocks that showed up in two or more of these mutual funds. Several of these companies showed up in at least five funds, and about a third of these were listed on the top-ten holdings by at least three different fund managers. (Presenting this summary of stocks does not constitute an expressed or implied endorsement of these companies or a recommendation to buy securities, but merely an example of how many fund managers select similar stocks for their small-cap portfolios.)

Garry Trudeau has recently produced, in his nationally known comic strip, a series that has followed the exploits of Mike Doonesbury and his new wife Kim as they try to launch a small Internet service company from their "Seattle-area" garage. As they begin to seek venture capital funding for their small-cap firm, Mike's daughter notes that the start-up is really "burning through a ton of money." Mike points out that they are positioning themselves to go public and that, for Internet businesses, "profitability is for wimps" because "it's okay to lose a lot of money, as long as it's on purpose."[19] Not every small-cap firm that actively pursues a niche in these markets will prove to be successful. Six years from now, mergers, acqui-

sitions, bankruptcies, and low-level profitability will ultimately characterize many of today's entrants; however, many well-screened stocks today
will prove incredibly successful in the future, and small-cap investors who
exercise patience and an "entrepreneurial perspective" will likely reap the
benefits that come with taking an equity stake in the value of potential
innovation.

TABLE 7–1   Selected Small-Cap Common Stocks

ICG Communications	Mercury Interactive	IMAX Corporation
Graham-Field Health	On Assignment, Inc.	Analogic
Products	Nymagic Insurance	Comfort Systems USA
Simon Transportation	Allied Waste Industries	Strayer Education
Safeguard Scientific	Orion Capital	MTS Systems
Valassis Communications	Applied Power, Inc.	Physician Reliance
	Network Appliance, Inc.	Network
Metzler Group, Inc.		
Universal Corp. Holding	Ames Dept. Stores	Granite Construction
Qlogic Corporation	Serologicals Corp.	Sofamor-Danek Group
Minimed, Inc.	Richfood Holdings	Pilgrims Pride
Cinar Films, Inc.	Parkway Properties	Corrections Corp. of
	SteriGenics International	America
Medicis Pharmaceutical		Glacier Bancorp
Meta Group, Inc.	Downey Financial	
NHC Corporation	CompX International	Tower Corp.
Hyperion Solutions	Holophane	Skytel Communications
Curtiss-Wright	Saville Systems	U.S. Foodservice, Inc.
		Mentor
Fremont General	SPS Technologies, Inc.	
Furniture Brands	Medialink Worldwide	Concord
Shopko Stores	American Italian Pasta	Communications
CEC Entertainment	Matthews International	EastGroup Properties
Metromedia Fiber	U.S. Foodservice	Summit Bancorp
		Interim Services, Inc.
Network, Inc.	Omnicare, Inc.	
Black Hills Corporation	Cablevision Systems	USA Networks, Inc.
Adelphia	Sterling Commerce	Total Renal Care, Inc.
Communications	Citizens Banking	Lexmark International
Aliant Communications	Caseys General Stores	Resmed, Inc.
A. O. Smith	Policy Mgmt. Systems	Hearst-Argyle
		Television, Inc.
Shorewood Packaging	TeleCom Liberty Media	
Coach USA	Network Appliance, Inc.	
Jabil Circuit, Inc.	Registry, Inc.	
Solectron Corp.	Key Energy Group	
Synopsys, Inc.	Tetra Tech	

Notes

1. See various issues of *Technology Review*, published by the Massachusetts Institute of Technology, 77 Massachusetts Avenue, Cambridge, MA 02139 (1997–1998).

2. *Technology Review*, May–June, 1998.

3. See various issues of *Money World*, published by Gulf-Atlantic Publishing, Inc., Winter Park, FL 32789 (1998).

4. See the Innovation Research Centre at The Michael DeGroote School of Business at McMaster University (Canada) Website at http://irc.mcmaster.ca/irc.

5. Marcial, Gene, 1998. "Helping Organ Transplants Take," *Business Week*, June 22, p. 188.

6. Lieberman, David, 1998. "Little Known Firm Goes After Realm of Interactive TV," *USA Today*, July 15, p. 6B.

7. Dunn, Ashley, 1998. "The Subspace Race," *Los Angeles Times*, July 13, pp. D1, D6.

8. Rynecki, David, 1998. "Hype Hot for Broadcast.com despite Red Flags," *USA Today*, July 16, p. 1B.

9. Reuters, 1998. "Broadcast.com Sets Record for 1st-Day Trading," *Los Angeles Times*, July 18, pp. D1–2.

10. See Arnst and Carey, 1998. "Biotech Bodies," *Business Week*, July 27, pp. 56–63.

11. "Model Behaviour," 1998. *Economist*, July 18, pp. 68–69.

12. "Sticking Together," 1998. *Economist*, June 27, p. 85.

13. "The 1997 All-America Research Team," *Institutional Investor*, October, pp. 77–170.

14. Bartholomew, Douglas, 1997. "Expanding Horizon," *Institutional Investor*, October, pp. 1–10.

15. Grant, Debra, 1997. "Knowing the Unknowable," *Institutional Investor*, November, pp. 151–152.

16. Ibid.

17. Ibid.

18. Ibid.

19. Trudeau, Garry, 1998. "Doonesbury" comic strip (syndicated), *Los Angeles Times*.

CHAPTER 8

Small-Cap Diversification

There is really no way to avoid some of the more quantitative issues related to small-cap investing. Things like risk factors, correlation coefficients, and asset allocation functions must be clearly understood within the context of the overall small-cap investment strategy. But it is possible to cover the basic concepts of risk and return in portfolio and still not lose touch with the practical applications of these kinds of analyses in determining stock selection and performance evaluation criteria. Diversification is in many ways a very complex topic, and there are several different styles the small-cap investor can implement in constructing a stock portfolio. There is no strategy that can completely eliminate the various risks that accompany the choice of small-cap stocks for inclusion in an investment program. However, there are numerous ways to reduce risk exposure along the risk-return frontier of the small-cap stock portfolio. This chapter further examines the concepts of risk and return that were introduced back in Chapter 1, and it relates these to specific strategies aimed at small-cap diversification.

Types of Risk

Earlier in the book, risk and expected return were shown to be directly related to each other. Figure 1–1 summarized the possible combinations of risk and expected return between a risk-free asset and a fully diversified market portfolio. Investors make decisions about the risk-return trade-off along a curve defined as the efficient frontier. Decisions about risk tolerance need to be examined as they relate to the prospects for a given investment return. The small-cap investor is confronted by two basic risks. The first is market risk, also known as *systematic* risk. This represents the impact that the broader overall market movements have on an investor's holdings. The second is business risk, also known as *nonsystematic* risk, or firm-specific risk, which explains the fluctuations in firm value that are attributable to the unique issues of the company. Product and service impact on customers in the target industry, financial structure, cash flow, the management team, and decision making, as well as the competition and future research and development issues are nonsystematic risks. The larger underlying market risks cannot be avoided very easily, if at all. *Macroeconomic* information about interest rates, foreign trade balances, expected inflation, production output, monetary policy, government spending policies, and employment figures affect a stock's variance.

No Escaping the Risk

The reality is this: small-cap investors cannot escape the impact that broad market movements may have on the return of any single stock in portfolio. This systematic risk will most likely explain, to some degree, a portion of the variance in the price of a given stock over time. The nonsystematic risk accounts for the remainder of the variance not captured by the movements in the broader, underlying market. But small-cap investors may be able to diversify away a good portion of this firm-specific risk through careful portfolio management. Balancing different companies' business risks could provide the small-cap investor with a hedge against sharp declines in the aggregate value of the portfolio, and more importantly, a decrease in the overall volatility of average price performance for the portfolio in general. Well-designed diversification can offset some of the portfolio's nonsystematic variance, that which is explained by the unique microeconomic issues particular to just that firm. There is, of course, no way to completely avoid risks, but the prudent small-cap investor can utilize several different strategies aimed at reducing risk exposure.

Basics of Diversification

Contemporary portfolio diversification strategies vary quite a bit. Some models are highly quantitative and use sophisticated computer programs to periodically rebalance the portfolio's stock holdings based on recent news and information about individual firms, the market, and the economy in general. This is a form of asset allocation that creates the most efficient portfolio mix based on *expected* risk and return. The role of portfolio diversification was formally introduced as an investment finance strategy nearly 50 years ago by Harry Markowitz. It proposed the following three basic tenets.

1. Expected return and riskiness are the two relevant issues.

2. Rational investors will always choose to hold efficient portfolios that either maximize expected return for a given level of riskiness or minimize riskiness for a given level of expected return.

3. Efficient portfolios can be identified by analyzing variations in returns for one stock compared to every other stock.[1]

How do these fundamental principles relate to the small-cap investment strategy? The small-cap investor can apply these basic concepts to construct various types of portfolios that will each have different objectives and rationales for use. Holding small-cap stocks in portfolio will first focus on the expected return of a given company, and the corresponding level of expected risk that accompanies that firm. Next, small-cap investors will either target a certain degree of risk and then maximize their return at that point, or they will target a given return and minimize their risk to obtain that. Finally, small-cap stocks can be analyzed to accomplish this type of portfolio, and this includes comparisons with other small-cap stocks, as well as with other mid-cap and large-cap stocks.

Price Volatility

The merits of diversification have been thoroughly tested for several decades in the investment finance and portfolio management fields. The premise is really quite simple. The risk associated with investing in a given stock is the degree of volatility in price fluctuations the stock will experience over time. The greater the volatility, the greater the risk. Now, there is no such thing as an absolute measure of the riskiness for a stock. But a close approximation of volatility is captured by the size of the standard deviation around the average return for a given time period. For example, if you had monthly returns for a stock over the last five years, you could calculate the average monthly return for each of those 60 months. If they were all relatively similar and fell within a narrow range of values, the standard deviation (plus or minus) around the average return for the entire five years would be small and you would consider that stock to have low volatility. However, if the range of returns covered a wide range of values, then the standard deviation (plus or minus) would be large and you would consider that stock to have high volatility.

The fundamental premise of diversification strategies is that all stocks share some degree of influence from the market (systematic risk) that is common to all companies that trade on the various exchanges. These macroeconomic factors impact every issue. But there are nonsystematic, or firm-specific, risks that are unique to each individual company. The portfolio manager believes that the distinctive characteristics of one stock will tend to offset the particular nature of another stock, so that when one company is experiencing a downturn in price, this might be countered by a different stock that is gaining in value during the same time period. One form of diversification is simply the process of grouping stocks together that have different levels of volatility, so that stocks with small standard deviations are placed in portfolio with stocks with larger standard deviations. The expectation is that the lower-volatility stocks will average out with the higher-volatility stocks and that the overall portfolio will experience an acceptable middle ground of overall volatility. Another, more widely held, form of diversification involves comparing how different pairs of stocks behave relative to each other and then placing into a portfolio those stocks with the least similarity in price movement.

Correlation

A correlation coefficient is a measure of how closely associated any two stocks are over the same time period.[2] For example, it is quite easy to take the historical prices of a stock and calculate the average return for, say, each month over the last five years, including the standard deviation around each average monthly return. This coefficient ranges between a *negative 100 percent* (–100% signals the strongest correlation—when one stock goes down in price the other tends to go up in price), through *zero* (the two stocks have zero correlation), up to *positive 100 percent* (+100% is also the strongest correlation, but this is where when one stock goes up, the other tends to do the same). When the coefficient measures closer to +100 percent or –100 percent, the two stocks move with the same magnitude. When the coefficient is somewhere between negative 100 percent up to zero, the two stocks tend to move in the opposite direction, but the magnitude of those movements is not similar. Also, from zero up to positive 100 percent, the two stocks tend to move in the same direction, but the size of the movements is not to the same degree. The basic strategy using the coefficient is to construct a portfolio by combining groups of uncorrelated stocks in order to provide some "opposite direction" and "different magnitude" effects between individual firms.

Beta

In the early 1960s, Stanford economist Bill Sharpe proposed that a correlation coefficient be calculated between the average monthly returns for any individual stock and the average monthly returns in the broader market for the same time period. This measure of correlation, called covariance (how did the stock covary with the market) would serve as an indicator of the movement of a given stock with the movement of the underlying market. Sharpe set up a ratio of this covariance compared to the size of the market's independent variance and called it *beta*.[3]

FORMULA

Small-Cap Stock's Beta =
Covariance of the Stock with the S&P 500 Index ÷
Variance of the S&P 500 Index

Note: The covariance measures how the stock and the market index moved relative to each other over the most recent 60 months; i.e., when one was up, was the other also up and to the same degree? Or when one was down, was the other also down and to the same degree? This comovement is compared to the market index by itself to see if the stock was more volatile, about the same, or less volatile than the broad market.

As a ratio, Beta provided investors with a very easy-to-use, practical tool that could be of help in the construction of a portfolio. Stocks that were correlated with the market could be *less* volatile than the market or *more* volatile than the market or they could have about the *same* level of volatility as the market. Other stocks tended to be uncorrelated with the market. Small-cap investors can use beta, as well as the correlation coefficient, to screen and select various stock issues for potential portfolio inclusion, depending upon their overall objectives, risk tolerance, and time horizon.

In the late 1960s, a classic investment finance study was published by John Evans and Stephen Archer dealing with the process and effects of diversification. They randomly selected 2400 different portfolios, composed of one stock, two stocks, three stocks, and so on all the way to 40 stocks, from the S&P 500 Index over a 10-year period of time. Evans and Archer found that the risk for each separate *random* portfolio was inversely related to the number of stocks that were included in the portfolio.[4] Figure 8–1 shows this relationship. The vertical axis measures the standard deviation (plus or minus) around the average return for a given portfolio, and the horizontal axis shows the number of individual stocks in the portfolio. When a small-cap investor holds just one stock, the standard deviation of that one stock is the portfolio's volatility. After the second stock is added to the portfolio, the standard deviation decreases significantly, as the two issues provide some degree of offset to each other's risks. The

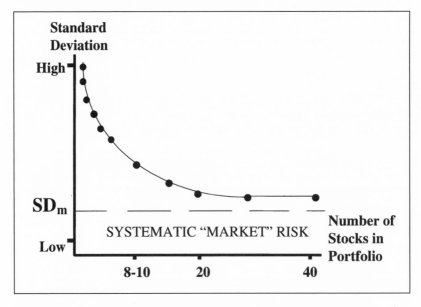

FIGURE 8–1   Random Diversification Is Limited to 20 to 30 Individual Stocks in Portfolio

third stock is added, as is the fourth and fifth and so on, and the overall standard deviation continues to decline. The dotted line (SD$_m$) shows the standard deviation for the underlying broader market. Somewhere around 8 to 10 stocks, the portfolio's standard deviation continues to be reduced, but at a decreasing rate. At around 20 stocks, the portfolio's standard deviation is experiencing only very small marginal decreases, and from that point out to the vicinity of 30 stocks, the portfolio's standard deviation becomes asymptotic (virtually parallel) to the standard deviation in the underlying market. So there is actually a point at which further diversification makes no sense.

Risk Reduction

Most small-cap investors do not really understand the different forms of risk reduction that can be accomplished through prudent diversification. These include: (1) a reduction in portfolio variance, (2) a measurable increase in expected return with only a small marginal increase (or no increase at all) in risk assumed, and (3) a measurable decrease in portfolio risk exposure with virtually no decrease in the portfolio's expected return. There is no way to guarantee that one diversification strategy will accomplish all three of these goals, but it is very likely that two of the three goals can be met at the same time. A measurable increase in expected return can often be secured with a disproportionately smaller increase (or no increase) in the risk assumed, and this can sometimes actually reduce the overall portfolio variance by a small measure. It is not difficult to reduce the overall risk exposure, and also reduce the portfolio's variance, while maintaining the aggregate expected return of the fund. Each of these maneuvers is subject to the unique market setting and company circumstances present at the time that trades are executed, but a close watch of the fundamentals can generate successful results.

The first goal of diversification is to reduce the overall volatility of the portfolio. This can be accomplished by balancing stocks that have larger standard deviations with issues that have smaller variances compared to their average return. The second goal is to periodically rebalance the portfolio to add stocks that have higher expected returns and yet very similar volatility to stocks already in the portfolio. This can happen when favorable new information is recently released about a small-cap firm and there

is an increase in forecasted earnings. The newly added issue might keep
the overall portfolio standard deviation relatively stable while at the same
time increase the prospects for strong capital appreciation.

The third goal involves rebalancing the portfolio with stocks that have
somewhat lower volatility compared to current holdings but with expected
returns that are very similar to existing company shares. Figure 8–2 summarizes the four basic configurations of a small-cap diversification strategy. The portfolio may develop a single-industry intraclass small-cap
profile, which is virtually a small-cap "sector" fund (e.g., all medical technology companies). The strategy could also create a multi-industry
intraclass small-cap profile, where the portfolio is composed of smaller
firms but is diversified across several different industries. Here the volatility character may begin (over time) to replicate the movement of the
NASDAQ composite index. The third profile creates a single-industry
interclass character, which again looks like a sector fund, but the small-
cap holdings are balanced with mid-cap and large-cap stocks. The final
combination sets up a multi-industry interclass investment schedule that
invests in the entire range of small-to-large cap firms across various industries. This could begin to replicate the movement of the broader stock
market (e.g., the S&P 500 Index). Each of these four small-cap diversification strategies will most likely produce an entirely unique portfolio vari-

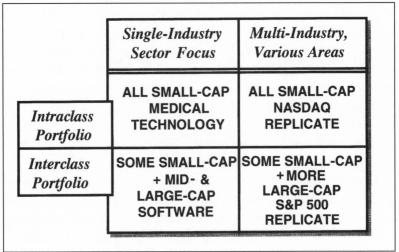

	Single-Industry Sector Focus	*Multi-Industry, Various Areas*
Intraclass Portfolio	ALL SMALL-CAP MEDICAL TECHNOLOGY	ALL SMALL-CAP NASDAQ REPLICATE
Interclass Portfolio	SOME SMALL-CAP + MID- & LARGE-CAP SOFTWARE	SOME SMALL-CAP + MORE LARGE-CAP S&P 500 REPLICATE

FIGURE 8–2   Small-Cap Diversification Strategies

ance, risk exposure, and expected return when compared to the other profiles. There can be no guarantee that one of these four strategies will produce the "best" or "better" relative investment performance over time, because of changes in macroeconomic, industry, and firm-specific fundamentals, as well as movements in the broader underlying market.

Single Industry Intraclass

Many investors believe that a measurable level of diversification can be accomplished simply by spreading portfolio dollars across a dozen or so firms across a given industry. For example, many small-cap investors want to focus on the entrepreneurial, fast-growth high-technology sectors of the market. They purchase stock in three retail software firms and one wholesale distributor, two multimedia companies, a few Internet communications businesses, a brand-new up-and-coming computer peripheral connections firm, and two international voice-data network companies. But that portfolio is probably not diversified to any measurable extent. The problem with this strategy is that even though each firm may in fact represent a different business and customer focus, they are all most likely related to the markets for computer-oriented products and services.

Diversification is never a function of an individual's interpretation of what might constitute similar or different industry groups. The only true measure of diversification is the level of correlation between the periodic returns of any two stocks over the course of the last several years (typically calculated over 60 months). Many investors naively assemble a collection of small-cap stocks into a portfolio and believe it will provide a hedge against certain types of risk exposure.

Multi-industry Intraclass

The first general form of small-cap diversification is called *intraclass diversification*. It is designed to spread the risk of the portfolio among various *categories* of small-cap stocks. These could include different companies from: (1) information systems, (2) computer hardware, (3) computer software, (4) telecommunications, (5) defense and aerospace subcontractors, and (6) consumer electronics industries. This strategy is uniquely intraclass because it places the entire portfolio holdings into small-cap common stocks, and diversification takes place across different industries, but all *within* the small-cap category of investment instruments. By utilizing this approach, small-cap investors can create what is essentially a sector fund, the sector being those firms with less than $1 billion in market capitalization (or some other predetermined threshold).

Interclass Single Industry

The second method of small-cap diversification is called *interclass diversification*. Its objective is to spread the risk of the portfolio *between* small-cap common stock and large-cap issues. Small-cap investors can organize various weights of small-cap stocks relative total portfolio value. These could be 50/50 (50 percent small-cap and 50 percent large-cap) or 75/25 (in favor of small-caps) or some other allocation based upon risk tolerance, expected returns, and the investment holding period. Evidence suggests that small-cap stocks can increase the compound returns in interclass diversified portfolios, even at times when the S&P 500 outperforms small-stock returns.[5]

Interclass Multi-industry

The fourth diversification strategy places small-cap stocks in a portfolio with shares from mid-cap and large-cap companies, and these various firms represent several different industries that are decidedly not correlated with each other. The expected outcome of this strategy is to simply allow small-cap stocks to contribute a degree of high-end upside potential to an otherwise "average risk" portfolio composition. Here investors generally believe they can put a relatively low proportion (say, 15 to 20 percent) of small-cap stocks alongside a broadly diversified portfolio of mid-cap and large-cap stocks. This is done in much the same way that options or index futures might be added to a traditional equity portfolio to provide a "speculative" component to an otherwise growth-oriented strategy. The problem here is that the small-cap stocks might be viewed only for their near-term upside potential, rather than for their extraordinary growth potential over the longer-term. In fact, these smaller, emerging ventures may have far better prospects for appreciation compared to the large-caps.

Examples of Diversification

The Standard & Poor's 500 Index is widely recognized as a broad measure of performance for the largest publicly traded American companies. In September of 1994, Dimensional Fund Advisors, Inc. compared small-cap stocks to the S&P 500 for the period from 1926 to 1992 and found that $1 invested in the S&P Index in 1926 would have grown to be worth $727.84, while $1 invested in small-cap stocks would be worth $1956.45. They also found that small-caps generated 168.8 percent additional growth in value during that time period (an annualized compounded return of 11.98 percent in small-cap stocks versus only a 10.34 percent in the S&P 500 Index). Back in Chapter 3, it was noted that the period of 1975 to 1983 is considered by many financial analysts to be an anomaly with regard to small-cap stocks outperforming large-cap companies. If 1975–1983 is removed from the calculation, a $1 investment in large-caps in 1926 would be worth only $195.24 (not $727.84), and $1 invested in small-caps would be worth only $138.65 (compared to $1956.45). In this comparison, large-caps outperformed small-caps by almost 41 percent additional growth in future value.

Other investment studies have also argued that the years 1984 to 1990 were also an uncharacteristic period of extraordinarily "hot" (hyper-growth) stocks featuring some of the fastest-growing IPOs in American history. When this hot-stocks period of the mid-to-late 1980s is removed, large-cap stocks yield $279.49 compared to small-caps at $1633.85. In that case, small-cap stocks greatly outperformed large-caps by an additional 485 percent growth in value. The period of 1975–1983 might be an anomaly, as this clearly shows that a case can be made that the extraordinary growth of the late 1970s and early 1980s was much more significant than the hot-stocks period of 1984–1990. Table 8–1 summarizes these returns.

Now, consider investing the same $1 for the same 67 years between 1926 and 1992 using an interclass small-cap diversification strategy of 50 percent invested in small-caps and 50 percent invested in the S&P 500 Index. Recall from Table 8–1 that a $1 investment in large-cap stocks yielded a $727.84 (10.34 percent annual compounded growth) and a $1 small-cap investment yielded a $1956.45 (11.98 percent annual compounded growth). The $1 invested with interclass diversification would have grown to $1690.78 (11.73 percent annual compounding), which is

TABLE 8–1　Comparison of Small-Cap and Large-Cap Investments Over Time

FUTURE VALUE OF $1 INVESTMENT

	1926–1992	1926–1992 (excl. '75–'83)	1926–1992 (excl. '84–'90)
S&P 500 Index	$727.84	$195.24	$279.49
Small-Cap Stocks	$1956.45	$138.65	$1633.85

PERCENTAGE RETURNS ANNUAL COMPOUNDING

	1926–1992	1926–1992 (excl. '75–'83)	1926–1992 (excl. '84–'90)
S&P 500 Index	10.34%	9.52%	9.84%
Small-Cap Stocks	11.98%	8.88%	13.12%

less than the straight small-cap investment but significantly higher than the large-cap investment alone. Remember that when the 1975–1983 period was removed, large-caps greatly outperformed the small-caps. But the 50–50 diversification between large-caps and small-caps would have grown to $225.65 in value (versus $195.24 for large-caps and only $138.65 for small-caps). The diversified holdings grew at 9.79 percent annual compounding versus 9.52 percent for large-caps, and just 8.88 percent for small-caps.

David Booth and Eugene Fama introduced the *return contribution measure* to determine the contribution that each asset makes to the overall return when two or more stocks are held together in portfolio. For the period from 1941 to 1990, they examined an intergroup diversification strategy using small-cap stocks with the S&P 500 Index and found that the return contribution of small-cap stocks is 1.36 percent higher than its compounded return, while the return contribution of the S&P 500 Index is just 0.41 percent higher than its compounded return.[6] This appears to show that small-caps may actually contribute much more to the overall return of the portfolio (95 basis points, or almost a full percentage point). This occurs because the intergroup diversification eliminates more of the variance of small-cap returns. When the small-cap investor effectively uses an inter-group diversification strategy, the performance of small-caps in a portfolio will always be much greater than simply calculating the separate compounded returns for each asset group.

Some Cautious Advice

There is no way to fully insulate the small-cap portfolio from daily, weekly, monthly, or quarterly volatility. In fact, whether the small-cap investor is concerned with intraday price movements or five-year market trends, diversification will never be a perfect insurance policy against downside effects on portfolio performance. However, traditional investment studies have shown quite conclusively that well-designed diversification strategies have, over longer periods of time, proved to be excellent ways to soften the downside impact of negative news from one or more sectors of the market. In the contemporary markets of late 1998, some of the established havens for diversification have lost some of their luster. For example, foreign markets are used to afford investors an excellent place to offset domestic (U.S.) market risk. Today, foreign stock markets are increasingly linked to domestic markets, so that negative news there has an almost immediate and direct impact here. This adverse effect is referred to as a *market contagion*, because the foreign information infiltrates the domestic market fundamentals. In a similar way, small-cap stocks have long been used as an instrument in portfolio to yield a level of global diversification. But small-cap companies are becoming increasingly more correlated with their large-cap counterparts, and with this, the benefits of diversification may already be decreasing. Although smaller firms are still less exposed in foreign markets than large-caps, current trends are starting to demonstrate that the gap between small-cap and large-cap exposure is narrowing.[7]

Notes

1. Markowitz, Harry M. , 1952. "Portfolio Selection," *Journal of Finance*, No. 7, March, pp. 77–91.

2. Fama, Eugene, 1976. *Foundations of Finance* (New York: Basic Books).

3. Sharpe, William F., 1963. "A Simplified Model for Portfolio Analysis," *Management Science*, No. 9, January, pp. 227–293.

4. Evans, John L., and Stephen H. Archer, 1968. "Diversification and the Reduction of Dispersion: An Empirical Analysis," *Journal of Finance*, Vol. 23, December, pp. 761–767.

5. Booth, D. G., and E. F. Fama, 1992. "Diversified Returns and Asset Contributions." *Financial Analysts Journal*, May–June.

6. Ibid.

7. Pradhuman, Staya, 1998. "Costs of Contagion," *The Financial Survey*, May–June, pp. 5–7.

chapter 9

Small-Cap
Asset Allocation

Having established the basic ground rules for small-cap diversification strategies in Chapter 8, the next step involves establishing objectives, risk factors, and trading rules for small-cap asset allocation. Whereas diversification is the underlying rationale that supports mixing various combinations of stocks in portfolio, small-cap asset allocation creates the methodology and decision parameters to implement the diversification strategy and maintain the targeted balance of various holdings in the small-cap portfolio.[1] The asset allocation process uses either an *active management* or *passive management* approach.[2] Although there are many similarities with the traditional forms of allocating funds among equities, fixed income, and liquidity (near-cash instruments), small-cap asset allocation is a unique method of managing diversification to match the overall goals and objectives of the portfolio over time. Allocation management style remains a major topic of debate in modern investment finance, in that evidence is still somewhat inconclusive as to whether it is possible for a portfolio manager to consistently outperform the market.[3]

Traditional Asset Allocation

There are several different ways that asset allocation is implemented in modern portfolio management. The strategy itself is rather simple. Investors configure their portfolios across three core categories of holdings: (1) equities, (2) fixed income, and (3) cash, which represents near-cash liquid instruments such as money market mutual funds, individual issues of commercial paper, banker's acceptances, repurchase agreements, secondary certificates of deposits (CDs), and U.S. Treasury bills.[4] The concept of asset allocation is not new, but the means to manage the portfolio's funds have changed dramatically over the last decade. Many forms of asset allocation are tied to proprietary computer programs specifically designed to balance portfolio holdings relative to a very precise performance objective, risk profile, and investment time horizon. Typically, fund managers split their money under management among three general categories of securities. The first category, *equities*, includes common stock with the primary emphasis on capital appreciation (as opposed to regular dividend distributions). The second group is composed of *income* instruments such as corporate bonds, intermediate and long-term U.S. Treasury issues (such as T-notes and T-bonds), government agency bonds (like GNMA, FNMA, and FHA securities), secondary mortgages and longer-term certificates of deposit, and corporate preferred stock.

Figure 9–1 summarizes and compares two asset allocation arrangements. Portfolio A is a typical portfolio configuration based upon a general growth-oriented performance objective. It is heavily weighted into equities. Investors would make this allocation based upon a certain risk tolerance and the anticipated holding period for the instruments in portfolio. This is compared to a typical asset allocation in the context of a small-cap investment strategy (portfolio B). It is also aimed at securing a specified level of risk exposure in the context of an expected holding period. Notice that in each case, the primary equity allocation is disproportionately greater than the secondary allocation and the cash component. This is the basis of asset allocation. The second- and third-level holdings provide a measure of overall portfolio risk reduction relative to the primary holdings.

In portfolio A, the strategy is aimed at taking advantage of equity returns buffered by other allocations. In portfolio B, the strategy is focused on small-cap stocks that are similarly buffered by other holdings. But recognize that fund A uses fixed-income items (government bonds and other corporate long-term debt) to offset the risk inherent in this traditional equity area. On the other hand, fund B uses large-cap and mid-cap

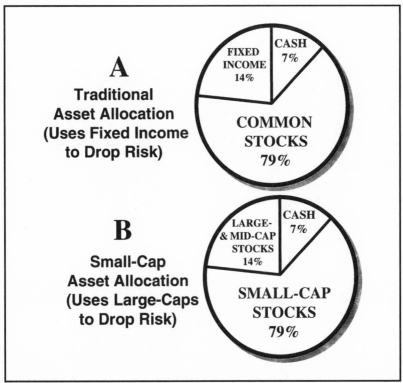

A

Traditional Asset Allocation (Uses Fixed Income to Drop Risk)

FIXED INCOME 14%

CASH 7%

COMMON STOCKS 79%

B

Small-Cap Asset Allocation (Uses Large-Caps to Drop Risk)

LARGE- & MID-CAP STOCKS 14%

CASH 7%

SMALL-CAP STOCKS 79%

FIGURE 9–1   Two Approaches to Asset Allocation

stocks to offset the risk inherent in the small-cap allocation. This is a significant issue directly related to small-cap asset allocation. The primary objective of traditional asset allocation is to balance the various risks for an overall targeted portfolio profile. Interest income from bonds, cash flow from dividends, and the liquidity of near-cash (short-term) money market instruments are commingled with the capital appreciation expectations of equity in order to arrive at an overall portfolio risk position that matches the investors' time horizon and risk tolerance. The primary objective of small-cap asset allocation is also to rebalance holdings on a periodic basis so as to update the portfolio because of changes in investor risk tolerance. However, the main difference is that this allocation is typically between small-caps and larger-cap stocks rather than between equities and income instruments, as is the case in traditional asset allocation.

Life-Cycle Allocations

Burton Malkiel's commentary dealing with the random and sometimes nonrespecting nature of stock portfolio compositions, says that asset allocation should probably be closely tied to the investor's particular stage in life, what he terms the "normal life cycle" of investing. His four stages of the investor's typical life cycle include: (a) Mid-20s (when capacity for risk is quite high), hold 70% in stocks, 25% in bonds, and 5% in cash; (b) age 30 to 40 (risk capacity shrinks at mid-life crisis), hold 60% stocks, 35% bonds, and 5% cash; (c) 50s (further reduce risk exposure), hold 50% stocks, 45% bonds, and 5% cash; (d) 60s and beyond (little or no capacity for risk), hold 60% bonds, 35% stocks, and 5% cash. This type of asset allocation targets a weighted risk exposure relative to an investor's remaining time frame for expected end results. As the investment horizon draws closer, tolerance for risk decreases.[5]

Asset Allocation Factors

Traditional asset allocation requires the portfolio manager to work from one of three different perspectives: (1) the valuation-based approach, (2) the cyclical considerations approach, or (3) a hybrid of the first two methods.[6] The first perspective views the portfolio's assets in light of whether they have become too expensive to hold (and should be sold) or whether they are still undervalued in the market (and should be held). The second perspective views the broad market movements (up and down) as cyclical and related to the bond market and interest rates. This means the portfolio will need to rebalance its holdings as the "normal" business cycle changes over time. The third method incorporates aspects from each of the first two, so that individual asset values are assessed in view of expectations generated by the current stage of the business cycle.

There are two underlying factors that directly affect the style and method of traditional asset allocation employed by investors. The first factor deals with the fund's stated objective with respect to the expected holding period. This is also referred to as the *investor's life cycle* as it pertains to performance objectives and the time horizon for the portfolio. The second factor addresses the risk tolerance of the investor. These two items will impact each other to some degree as well. For example, an investor with a longer-term approach to holding securities in portfolio may very well be willing to accept greater risk, due in part to the length of the time horizon involved. This is not always the case, however. Someone with a long time horizon could still be very risk-averse and expect to minimize exposure to price fluctuations as much as possible by locking in to a dependable stream of income. On the other hand, an investor with a relatively short time horizon does not necessarily want to emphasize lower risk exposure. Shorter-term investment objectives may actually target more risk in the hope of realizing a significant capital appreciation because of a perceived timing issue in the market or with a certain company.

Many investors often mistake a shorter holding period as being synonymous with lower risk exposure, because there exists a need for reliable income on a quarterly or monthly basis. But this is not always the case. The asset allocation process cuts across the investment horizon and risk tolerance in several ways. Figure 9–2 shows the various relationships between these two dimensions as they relate to common stock portfolios. Area A represents the place of traditional blue-chip large-cap stocks. These have risks that are for the most part similar to the underlying market, and the investment horizon is generally greater than one year, up to around five years. Area B describes the domain of small-cap stocks based upon the entrepreneurial perspective presented in this book. Area C represents fixed income instruments that are typically less volatile than large-cap equities. Area D shows the place for shorter-term speculative products like commodities futures contracts and stock options. Area E represents

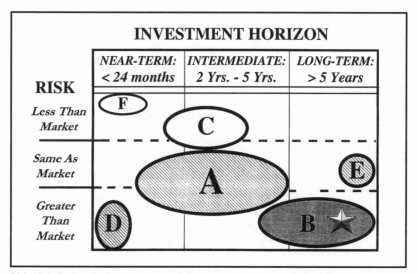

FIGURE 9–2   Relationship of Risk and Stock Holding Periods

some of the higher-yielding bonds that may require investors to hold for a longer time period. And area F captures the low-risk (no-risk) portion of the portfolio allocated to near-term money market instruments (cash).

Small-cap asset allocation blends the portfolio holdings to accomplish a given level of portfolio risk exposure for a given time horizon. What makes it so unique from traditional asset allocation strategies is that the fund seeks to balance equities (small-cap stocks) with more equities (large-cap stocks). This is based on the belief that the small-caps have unique risk-return profiles and longer expected holding periods when compared to large-cap stocks. The large-caps and mid-caps are folded into the portfolio to provide a risk reduction effect to the primary fund holdings, the small firms. It is important to note that this style of allocation will in fact reduce the overall risk exposure profile of the small-cap portfolio (the large-caps will accomplish this). However, the overall portfolio risk position will still be higher than a fund with primary holdings in large-cap stocks that uses fixed-income securities (bonds and such) to achieve risk reduction through asset allocation. In each case, asset allocation accomplishes the task of risk specification for the fund. But large-cap portfolios probably start with a much lower initial risk position compared to the small-cap portfolio. So even if both funds were able to achieve a 10 percent overall risk reduction relative to the time horizon, the end result will likely show that the small-cap portfolio has a higher risk relative to the large-cap fund. Can small-cap investors still approach a comparable level of overall risk exposure like a large-cap fund? Of course they can. This could happen if the individual small-cap holdings were reduced in the portfolio, but when this occurs, the fund may no longer look like (or truly be) a small-cap portfolio. The key to small-cap asset allocation is accepting the higher level of risk exposure.

Small-Cap Allocation Targets

The process of asset allocation should be aimed at achieving a targeted overall risk exposure for the small-cap portfolio. Where traditional allocation seeks to balance equity, income, and cash, small-cap allocation is focused on two potential targets. The first is liquidity-oriented (the time horizon) and the other is cash-flow oriented (the volatility of the stock). These do not necessarily have to be mutually exclusive, but they are somewhat related. Small-cap investors will need to stay actively involved in monitoring the status of the portfolio's holdings, especially during times of increased upside or downside price movements. It is during times of significant short-term fluctuations that the small-cap portfolio is most vulnerable to changes in its relative risk exposure and composition. An original strategy aimed at certain targets of risk and time horizon can be altered quite a bit simply because the stocks in the portfolio have experienced major price swings. There are numerous combinations of asset allocation programs that can emphasize the liquidity preference over the cash-flow expectations, and vice versa. But small-cap asset allocation can incorporate features from each of these targets into what amounts to a hybrid strategy aimed at either capital accumulation or capital conservation. The most important aspect for the small-cap investor is to recognize the unique firm profiles of smaller capitalization companies versus their large-cap and mid-cap counterparts. Like it or not, small-cap investing will never be (and should not be thought of as) the same strategy as traditional equity investing.

Allocation Variations

It can be difficult and frustrating to achieve either of the specific targets described in the previous section. The application of purchasing and monitoring tactics for individual stocks or small-cap mutual funds to one of these two allocation targets may not always be implemented in all cases of portfolio management. Small-cap investors must also recognize that any asset allocation mix is likely to rebalance itself over time due to normal fluctuations in the underlying market and changes in share prices. This means that some sections of the small-cap portfolio will increase in value faster or slower than other areas, thus creating different proportional dollar values in the relative allocation categories over time. At first glance, this might not seem to be a problem. But consider that each form of asset allocation produces a different overall risk profile for the small-cap portfolio or fund. Left unattended for just a few short years, a small-cap asset allocation common stock investment could easily take on an entirely new risk profile with respect to price volatility and expected return. For example, Table 9–1 shows how passive management over the last five years (1993–1998) would have produced a significantly different small-cap portfolio due entirely to the random price movements of the market.[7]

TABLE 9–1   Changes in Portfolio Risk Profile from 1993 to 1998

Year	Investment Category	Asset Allocation	Category Change
1993	Large-cap stocks	45%	
	Small-cap stocks	15%	
	Intermediate bonds	25%	
	Money market	15%	
	Overall risk position	**22%**	
1998	Large-caps	60%	*Increased by 33%*
	Small-cap stocks	15%	*Same proportion*
	Intermediate bonds	16%	*Decreased by 30%*
	Money market	9%	*Decreased by 40%*
	Overall risk position	**26%**	***Increased by 18%***

Small-cap investors must understand that asset allocation will effectively take place "with or without you," based solely on the random movements of the underlying market over time. An active role in the asset mix of the portfolio can accomplish a relatively stable mix of risk exposure and investment horizon. The small-cap asset allocation strategy should be reviewed periodically (this author recommends every six months) so that the portfolio holdings can be reallocated in order to rebalance the risk-time horizon interaction.

Small-Cap Allocation Over Time

The last issue that must be addressed involves how to rebalance the small-cap portfolio over the course of the investor's life cycle. It all begins with matching the stock screening process to the long-term entrepreneurial perspective for holding emerging, and potentially fast-growth, companies in portfolio. Refer back to Figure 9–1. As discussed, the small-cap segment of the market is inherently unique from large-cap equities. Establishing a certain risk profile for the small-cap portfolio is limited in some respects to the nature of the holdings. The portfolio is focused on small-cap stocks, so the profile cannot match a traditional "blue-chip" equity fund with similar percentages of holdings in the asset allocation strategy. What will most likely occur over time is that some of the primary small-cap holdings will no doubt experience a decrease in price volatility as they grow and mature in their respective industries. Others will remain in a certain risk class, and some may even become more risky. The key portfolio action will be to keep new small-caps coming into the portfolio on a regular basis. Some of these will replace the risk component that was reduced when a prior small-cap turned into a mid-cap or large-cap over time. Some of these will help to balance the increased risk component due to a prior holding's increased price instability over time.

Small-cap investors must take an active role in monitoring the risk and valuation horizons of the individual stocks held in portfolio. And even with a close watch on the ever-changing economy, the various industries represented, and the constant updates in the firm-specific information, active management and periodic rebalancing cannot guarantee that the small-cap portfolio will outperform the broader market for a given time period. A great example of this (but embarrassing for the fund managers) occurred in 1994, when *none* of the 50 Paine-Webber mutual funds offered to the public showed a positive return.[8] Or think about how during the first two quarters of 1995, only 226 of the more than 1850 growth stock mutual funds that receive regular coverage from Lipper Analytical Services (actively managed to some extent) were able to outperform the passively managed S&P 500 Index.[9] That means that only about one out of every eight stock funds had a successful strategy in place for that time period. Certainly, beating the broader market indexes is better examined over longer periods of time. But the fact remains that there is no way to know exactly what form of asset allocation and periodic rebalancing will generate the best returns over the long term. Small-cap investors must be willing to set their investment horizons for at least five years and accept the increased near-term volatility that comes with holding smaller, lesser-known stocks. Maintaining a targeted risk-return time frame will provide a measure of consistency in evaluating when to sell existing stocks and when to add new issues to the portfolio.

Notes

1. Good, W., R. Mernasen, and T. Barnaby, 1986. "Opportunity: Actively Managed Investment Universes," *Financial Analysts Journal*, January–February, pp. 17–21.

2. Fielitz, B., and F. Muller, 1983. "The Asset Allocation Decision," *Financial Analysts Journal*, July–August, pp. 45–50.

3. Dunn, P., and R. Theisen, 1983. "How Consistently Do Active Managers Win?" *Journal of Portfolio Management,* Summer, pp. 47–50.

4. See Chapter 1 of Arnott, R. and F. Fabozzi (eds.), 1992. *Active Asset Allocation* (Chicago: Probus Publishing).

5. Malkiel, Burton, 1990. *A Random Walk Down Wall Street* (New York: W.W. Norton), pp. 357–358.

6. Weigel, E., 1991. "The Performance of Tactical Asset Allocation," *Financial Analysts Journal*, September–October, p. 63.

7. McNamee, Mike, 1998. "Commentary: Personal Business," *Business Week*, August 3, p. 94.

8. Kahn, V., 1995. "Dysfunctional Families," *Smart Money*, August, pp. 107–114.

9. Waggoner, J., 1995. "Why Most Mutual Funds Lag the S&P 500," *USA Today*, July 6, p. B1.

Putting It All Together

10

Small-Cap
Portfolio Samples

How the Fund Managers Do It

S mall-cap investing is not an exact science. There is no officially recognized *way* to do it. All small-cap investors and fund managers approach the small-cap portfolio from a slightly different angle and incorporate their own unique set of guidelines and trading strategies. It is important to recognize statements, rationales, and policy commitments that reflect a true "entrepreneurial perspective" regarding investments in small-cap stocks. Diversification strategies and asset allocation priorities can vary greatly from one small-cap portfolio to another. There is no "cookie-cutter format" for structuring a fund's holdings. The investment time horizon is generally long-term oriented, focusing on five- to-seven years out into the future. But there can even be slight differences here as well, with some managers looking for a quicker turnaround in a given stock's performance.

The seasoned small-cap fund manager understands very well that the name of the game is completely based upon using a risk-weighted diversification among numerous promising small-cap stocks. Some stocks selected will perform fairly well, others will have marginally acceptable performance, and others will be disastrous. But the very best performing small-cap funds are generally dependent on between just three to five superstar companies that literally carry the portfolio's impressive aggregate return. Figure 10-1 depicts the typical percentage breakdown of small-cap stocks held in a fund. A manager holding 40 separate firms in the portfolio

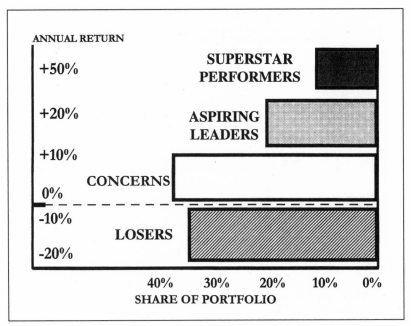

FIGURE 10–1   Expected Performance Within the Small-Cap Portfolio

will have on average eight aspiring leaders earning around 15 to 25 percent returns, 16 stocks that will cause concern (they're neither big winners or losers) with near-zero or single-digit returns, and maybe 12 that are performing quite poorly (negative returns). However, the four superstars might be averaging 50 to 75 percent each and together provide enough influence that the portfolio's overall return is above a 20 percent annual yield. Fund managers are not surprised by this. In fact it is fully anticipated. This is very similar to the way that most venture capital firms view their funding schedule of emerging companies. They know that for every ten firms in which they take an investment position, two will have "good" performance, four will be questionable, three will probably lose money, but one will provide extraordinary growth and help to carry the fund's overall return performance. So too, individual small-cap investors should recognize that their portfolio return will likely be distributed in much the same way.

Personal perspectives and the interpretation of public information are both subject to individual biases. The relative value of any given portfolio structure is based on the anticipation of future firm performance, earnings and cash flow, market expectations, and forecasted industry and macro-economic trends. Short-term volatility (price fluctuations) will always be present when holding equities in portfolio. Patience coupled with an undaunted entrepreneurial perspective toward the future are the necessary hallmarks to look for in a small-cap strategy. Uncovering hidden value and accepting the risks that typically accompany relatively "unproven" public companies are what make small-cap investing such a rewarding endeavor. The merit of any small-cap portfolio strategy will ultimately be its performance over the intermediate- to long-term horizon. The following sections highlight some of the portfolio positions, or types of funds, established by leading small-cap fund managers, and the motives, rationales, and philosophies that drive the investment strategies in this highly intriguing segment of the capital markets.[1]

Types of Small-Cap Funds

There are numerous small-cap investment funds in the United States. Table 10–1 provides a basic outline of the various categories of funds that are generally available from the major institutional investor groups. The semantics between different small-cap investment philosophies may appear to be, in one sense, overly particular in its references, and yet in another sense just different adjectives describing identical small-cap firm profiles. There may in fact be more than a dozen categories of small-cap investments. But the following list is arguably the basic summary of small-cap portfolios.

Penny Stocks

Perhaps the most speculative approach to small-cap investing involves investing in companies that are generally at the very smallest end of the market capitalization range. Nicknamed *penny stocks* because investors can often purchase them for just 5 or 10 cents per share, these companies are typically very obscure in their respective industries and lacking in any semblance of reliable information about firm operations, financial position, or senior management. Where most public companies at least trade

TABLE 10–1 Types of Small-Cap Funds

Small-Cap Fund Category	Primary Risk Assessment	Stock Focus or Investment Agenda
Penny stocks	Highly speculative	Accumulate tiny, undervalued, undiscovered companies. Cash in when the masses want it.
Emerging growth	High risk	Companies with innovative products and services, research capabilities, or other unique attributes. Firms that are "less familiar" to investors.
International	High risk	Newly formed, newly issued foreign firms in established industries. Currency fluctuations and market and political instability are added features.
Science and technology	High risk	Specific emphasis on computer hardware and software, bio-medical, telecommunications, and precision instruments.
Special equities	High risk	Companies making a major turnaround from negative to positive, also successfully emerging from bankruptcy.
Value	Above average risk	Firms in "good businesses" with significant entry barriers to limit new competition. Growing free cash flow, high return on capital.
Index funds	Above average risk	The simple, low-cost way to invest in small-caps.
Equity income	Near-average risk	Current dividend income and capital appreciation.

over-the-counter on the NASDAQ, these tiny companies can only be found among the "pink sheets." These quarterly (and sometimes only semiannual) reports summarize the trading "activity" (if it can be called that) in penny stocks. A quick perusal of the pink sheets will often show that many of these stocks have only two or three trades per quarter, and some only one trade per year. The issuing company may have just $2 million in assets (sometimes composed of just a capped oil well or raw land holdings) financed with $1 million in long-term debt. If the firm has 500,000 shares of stock outstanding, they might have sold on their last trade (eight months ago) at one cent per share. The quintessential stock speculator is hoping that when the oil well is sold to a large refinery, or the land is acquired by a major real estate developer, the shares will be worth eight or nine cents per share, which will generate a huge return to investors with the foresight to see early value. But penny stocks are really not the same as micro-caps ($50 million to $300 million in market capitalization) or traditional small-caps ($300 million up to $1 billion). The literal absence of any secondary information about the firm together with the overwhelming lack of any kind of trading liquidity make penny stocks a highly speculative and unique investment. Very few individuals, and virtually no institutional funds, make the pink sheets part of their small-cap investment strategy.

Emerging Growth

Perhaps the most exciting form of small-cap investing is focused on companies at the forefront of the truly innovative and emerging growth industries. These are entrepreneurial firms that have carved out a niche in what appears to be a high potential growth market. New products and services are reshaping sales, manufacturing, financial, or operations positions in the competitive marketplace. These companies are generally considered "overlooked" by the larger, institutional investors. Although the vast majority of these up-and-coming industries are watched closely by top-tier investment houses, there is a great deal of latitude available in evaluating individual companies within the industry and their relative merits for growth. Most professional fund managers believe that the "bottom-up approach" of screening basic investment fundamentals is the best way to locate extraordinary investment opportunities.

John Hancock Emerging Growth
Bernice Behar is a senior vice-president and portfolio management team leader for the John Hancock Emerging Growth Fund, whose stated objective is to "seek and identify small- and medium-sized companies that are growing faster than the overall business segment. Her management team is also looking for strong fundamentals such as: outstanding long-term growth prospects, a debt-free or low-debt balance sheet, improving profitability ratios, and a high degree of management ownership."[1]

International

Many fund managers pursue their small-cap probes out beyond the borders of the domestic U.S. stock markets. They believe that there are equally enticing investment opportunities among small-cap firms in Asian, Latin American, European, and Canadian markets. The screening criteria are, for the most part, very similar to the emerging growth factors used in analyzing domestic stocks. However, there are two unique issues that must be added to the risk assessment process when perusing potential foreign investments. First, many foreign markets are not as efficient in their pricing mechanisms for publicly traded shares of common stock. The bid-ask spread can be much wider than even the domestic small-cap spread. Reliable information may not be disseminated as widely or as quickly among market participants, which can contribute to less continuity in price movements both intraday and overnight. Second, the foreign shares must be purchased in the local currency. This additional risk affects accurate pricing and the timing of currency translation for cash flows on the front end at purchase, on the back end at the sale, and on any dividend income paid out to investors.

Acorn International Small-Cap
Leah J. Zell is the lead portfolio manager of Acorn International and coportfolio manager of Wagner European Smaller Companies Fund. The fund invests in stocks of small- and medium-sized companies outside the United States and includes risks not associated with investing in the United States, including currency fluctuations and possible political, economic, and social instability. As of the Fall 1998, the fund held such small-cap companies as WM Data (Sweden), Tieto Corp. (Finland), Rhoen Klinikum (Germany), Autogrill (Italy), Venture Manufacturing (Singapore), and Atos (France).[2]

Science and Technology

Many small-cap investments are configured much like sector funds, in that they have a very singular focus on just two or three closely related industries that deal with similar (or tangent) interrelated product and service applications. The typical science and technology (SAT) small-cap fund emphasizes silicon and other forms of microchip development, computer hardware and software programs, all aspects of satellite and wireless telecommunications, voice-data relay interfacing, medical innovations, and biochemical research and development companies. There are obviously many other industries where small-cap companies offer exceptional growth opportunities. However, many of the fastest-growing product and service markets happen to be in the physical and natural sciences (such as biological and chemical engineering) as well as all the various components of modern computing, communications, and instruments design. Again, there is no guarantee that SAT stocks will outperform non-SAT stocks over a given time period. Simply be aware that many of the best performers in recent times have been firms with SAT profiles. But like any market segment, the SAT area also has plenty of stories about terrible performers that were in the wrong technology at the time of transition in a major industry.

Special Equities

There are numerous definitions as to what constitutes a "special situation" for a publicly traded company. Small-cap stock funds that emphasize investment in these types of companies believe that after certain legal and economic circumstances have negatively impacted a firm's share price for a time, the company will rebound and subsequently create extraordinary investment opportunities for fund managers. The rationale is that these stocks will be able to dramatically turn their situation around for the better, and investors who own the stock prior to the turnaround will be handsomely rewarded for their foresight and patience. There is no guarantee that firms expected to turn around their internal and external financial turmoil will offer better upside potential than other small-cap stocks. Some may be successful, and others may not.

Value Funds

The typical small-cap value fund works very much the same way as the many large-cap value funds available in the market. The only difference is of course the size of the firms held in portfolio. Value investing is squarely aimed at uncovering those stocks that are supposedly grossly undervalued with respect to traditional fundamental analysis. This is different than looking for firms that are relatively new on the investment scene and are poised for growth in an emerging industry. The "value" concept involves finding firms that typically have had stronger past performance, but for a variety of reasons are considered to be on the down side, of a down trend, in a down segment, or of a down industry. Most of the investment community has felt that the company's debt position and interest payments threaten profitability and positive after-tax cash flow. Or, the analysts have been "cool" to the product and service markets' initial reception of recent offerings made by the firm. The fund manager's focus is aimed at finding excellent companies that have relatively low P/E ratios and/or market-to-book ratios which are not indicative of the "true expectations" for the company. Supposedly some small-cap fund managers believe that they can then translate this strategy toward a pool of smaller firms that fit the same descriptions for being *undervalued*. The difficulty comes in differentiating normal growth potential in one stock from an undervaluation in another stock. It could easily be argued that any stock that grows significantly over time must have been undervalued prior to the recent takeoff. Small-cap investors must be careful to not think that value investing is all that unique from screening strong growth candidates from among a qualified pool of small-cap companies.

Dreyfus Small-Cap Value

Peter Higgins is the lead portfolio manager for the Dreyfus Small Company Value Fund, whose objective is capital appreciation by investing in publicly traded equity securities of domestic and foreign issuers which are characterized as "value" companies, namely firms that exhibit very low market trading values relative to the underlying book value of the stock.[3] The focus is set on uncovering small companies that have been neglected by traders, but whose book value and earnings forecasts appear strong in the next few years.

Index Funds

Significant achievements have occurred in the financial markets' product offerings over the last two decades. The ability to trade common stock indexes has opened up an entirely new alternative to diversification and asset allocation strategies. Many investors are quite content to earn exactly what a widely watched index earns, rather than venture off into the realm of individual company stock ownership. Many of the small-cap index funds on the market today have actually created their own internal small-cap index by establishing a portfolio made up of shares from a wide range of other small-cap mutual funds. The investor is really buying into a combined "weighted average" of several small-cap portfolio management strategies, rather than a schedule of investments in a few dozen individual small-cap companies. In either case, a small-cap index fund is not inherently better than any other portfolio strategy aimed at capturing small-cap growth potential over time. In fact, it could be argued that this form of "aggregate composite investing" actually lacks a clearly defined vision and purpose for portfolio inclusion of assets.

Schwab Small-Cap Index Funds

Cynthia Liu is a senior mutual fund manager for Charles Schwab, Incorporated, and oversees the Schwab Small-Cap Index Fund, which is specifically designed to track the Schwab Small-Cap Index, which "represents the second-largest 1000 publicly traded U.S. companies, based on market capitalization. As a result of the changing values in the index, there was a 40% turnover in the stocks that comprise the index (in 1998), [and] since the fund seeks to track the index as closely as possible, significant rebalancing of the fund's portfolio was necessary."[4] Rather than hold a risk-specific asset allocation, the fund manager simply parallels the risk profile of the small-cap index.

Rather than research the fundamentals on specific companies expected to make a huge impact in their respective industries over the next several years, fund managers and shareholders have simply tried to accrue incremental bits of benefits from a wide variety of different (and maybe opposing) opinions about which are the very best small-cap stocks at a given time.

Equity Income

The typical equity-income fund uses small-cap stocks as a speculative portion of the equities component in the portfolio's asset mix. The small-caps are often not the primary holding of the fund. The manager will emphasize large-cap and mid-cap stocks, many of which pay consistently strong quarterly dividends. The small-cap holdings provide what the fund prospectus describes as "some upside potential" for significant growth. However, this small-cap portion of the fund is viewed as an upside diversification strategy (it *increases* the marginal risk exposure of the fund). In many ways these types of funds are not truly small-cap funds in the purest definition. These smaller companies are not viewed as a singularly viable investment area in and of themselves, but rather as high-end risk positions that offer some "potential" for extraordinary growth to increase the portfolio's overall return during the best of times. However, the manager's emphasis is still aimed at capital appreciation and reinvested dividends from larger, more established companies, many of which are components of major stock indexes.

Summary

Individual investors with a minimum capital base of around $50,000 can probably set up their own small-cap portfolio as part of an overall strategy aimed at growth during the long term. If the typical small-cap is trading for around 40 to 60 percent of the average stock price on the NYSE (say, around $12–$15 per share), and shares are purchased in standard round lots (100 shares), then $50,000 would be able to assemble a small-cap portfolio of around 35 separate companies. This fund would be somewhat equally weighted among the various shares represented, but it could then take on any one of the various target profiles discussed in this chapter. Even at $25,000 invested, a small-cap fund could be configured with around 20 different stocks. However, the opportunities in small-cap investing are less attributable to the amount of funds allocated and clearly a function of the "fund philosophy" employed by the small-cap investment manager.

Management Philosophies

The opening line of every small-cap fund prospectus introduces the manager's personal underlying rationale for investing in small-cap stocks.

It is crucial that the small-cap investor be very clear as to what the long-term objective, the intermediate- and near-term goals, and the underlying rationale are before any funds are committed to the individual portfolio or mutual fund. Small-cap fund managers also have a track record of relatively high turnover with respect to their duties as lead manager of a portfolio. During the course of the research and reporting for this book, it was discovered that there were only four small-cap fund managers from among more than three dozen examined, that had greater than five years management experience with the small-cap fund for which they were currently responsible. That is only about one in every 10 (11 percent), and that speaks loudly to the issue of whether the long-term perspective of the fund manager matches the objective and goals of the small-cap investor. In many cases the portfolio contains "inherited" stocks selected by a previous manager, some of which may be inconsistent with the present management philosophy. Small-cap investors should be very careful to understand the specific fundamental factors and influences that will guide the buy, sell, and hold decisions, whether in their own portfolio or in a public fund.

Specific Small-Cap Philosophy

Edgar Larsen is a senior portfolio manager for AIM Funds, and heads the selection process of small-cap stocks for several AIM mutual funds. The management philosophy at AIM states that "the Fund will devote a significant portion of its assets to 'micro-cap' stocks, those with market capitalization less than $250 million. About half the fund will be in small-cap stocks, with the other half in micro-caps . . . which are typically regional firms or start-ups developing a product line . . . [because] less news [means] more potential; [when] fewer analysts follow micro-cap companies, the scarcity of information gives our team a greater chance to shine."[5]

Notes

The information presented in this chapter represents four manila folders filled with printouts and prospectuses from more than 50 separate small-cap funds. Some of the data were downloaded directly from the various broker-dealer Websites, some came from the mailings that were sent to me when I requested information on these funds, and some came from discussions with over a dozen fund managers who typically requested anonymity with respect to citations. There exists a wealth of information across all types of fund philosophies. Individual managers bring their own personal biases to the stock selection and asset allocation processes. For obvious reasons, no individual managers were singled out for their personal small-cap philosophy or recent choices of investments.

1. See www.jhancock.com for fund holdings, management profile, and objectives.

2. See www.acornfunds.com for fund holdings, management profile, and objectives.

3. See www.dreyfus.com for fund holdings, management profile, and objectives.

4. See www.schwab.com for fund holdings, management profile, and objectives.

5. See www.aimfunds.com for fund holdings, management profile, and objectives.

CHAPTER 11

Frequently Asked Questions About Small-Cap Strategy

The prospects for initiating a small-cap investment strategy are quite promising, and yet the process and logistics can be somewhat complicated, and perhaps even difficult, to coordinate and implement. There are more than 2000 publicly traded companies with small-cap common stock market valuations under $1 billion. And each quarter, dozens of up-and-coming firms make initial public offerings (IPO) of common stock that raise, on average, around $35 million to $70 million in new investment capital. These IPOs may represent some of the very best opportunities for small-cap investors to participate in a true ground-floor opportunity. But the task of locating emerging industries and then screening for the firms with the greatest investment growth potential is not an exact science. Small-cap investors must develop and exercise a well-honed discretion so as to balance the quantitative and qualitative fundamentals about the economy, an industry, and a given firm. Not all aspects of the financial analysis and due diligence will yield a perfectly defined list of stocks that are all set for exceptional growth. Many of the measures require subjective interpretations and special insights about how the entirety of the factors and data come together to accurately describe a particular small-cap company profile. The track record for small-caps has proved to be quite impressive over the last seven decades. The contemporary market is replete with a wide range of smaller firms in dozens of emerging industries from which to choose. And the future promises that some of today's obscure companies will likely be the stock market performance stars of tomorrow. The remainder of this chapter addresses some of the most common questions pertaining to the entrepreneurial small-cap investment strategy.

The "Big" Picture of Small-Caps

No matter how many questions are posed with respect to small-cap investing, the basic answer will ultimately come back full circle to the most fundamental of the underlying issues that pertain to small-cap investing. Whether questions deal with portfolio rebalancing and asset allocation, IPOs, foreign versus domestic stocks, or the screening process compared to large- and mid-cap stocks, the most important aspect of small-cap stock investing is to recognize that there is no such thing as a perfect "system." Selecting companies, diversifying risk exposure, and holding during volatile short-term fluctuations all require patience, an entrepreneurial perspective, and a clear understanding that not all small caps will produce extraordinary returns. There is no "fast-track" to wealth creation through small-cap investing. There are many who will even dispute the potential of the small-cap performance edge when compared to larger company stocks. Perseverance and risk tolerance for the long haul will enter into almost every answer for the questions posed by potential investors.

Does Firm Size Matter?

The question of whether firm size is related to investment performance has been examined in significant detail since 1980. The first issue deals with the definition of "size." It can mean several things. Companies can be categorized based upon: (a) the value of common stock market capitalization, (b) the book value of the common stock, (c) the value of the assets, or (d) annual sales revenues. Strong evidence has been found to support the rationale that small firms, measured by market capitalization of equity, typically generate higher returns than mid-cap and large-cap companies.[1] Some believe that because small-cap firms are inherently riskier than mid-cap and large-cap firms, the apparently superior returns they earn are actually not all that extraordinary because they are simply providing a very high return that corresponds to their high level of risk.[2] Others argue that the size of the firm is not the most important issue, because the risk of small-cap firms is different in January than the remaining 11 months of the year. This means that small-cap companies have higher expected returns at the beginning of the year, so the small-cap premium disappears after factoring in the risk of the stock.[3] The price-to-book ratio has also been found to be a proxy for the market capitalization of a company, so that stocks with small price-to-book ratios generally tend to be small-cap stocks, and these earn higher returns than large price-to-book and large-capitalization stocks.[4]

Is Good Information Available?

The market for accumulating and tracking precise and current fundamental information about small-cap stocks is not as sophisticated as it is for mid-cap, and especially large-cap companies. There are several sources that keep track of IPOs,[5] and several good small-cap newsletters and Websites,[6] but this segment of the market does not attract nearly the attention for fundamental analysis that mid-cap and large-cap stocks enjoy from services such as the *Moody's Industrial Manual*, the *Value Line Investment Survey*, the *Standard & Poor's Stock Guide*.

Who Has First Access to IPOs?

Every small-cap investor would love to have the opportunity to purchase shares in an IPO at the opening bell the morning the stock goes public. A $10,000 investment in Yahoo! at the IPO in 1996 would today (July 1998) be worth $1.68 million.[7] Small-cap investors can stay in touch with recently issued, and pending, stock offers through specific tracking services such as the *IPO Reporter, Securities Data Incorporated*, the *IPO Financial Network*, and the *IPO Monitor*. But the introductory public market for IPOs is not a normal trading scenario. The lead underwriter of the IPO is an investment bank that has previously negotiated a set offering price for the shares with the business-going public. This price is printed in the final version of the prospectus filed with the Securities and Exchange Commission on the morning of the offer. That price is firm only as it relates to the capital actually received by the issuing company, called *the proceeds*. The proceeds are equal to the contractual offer price from the prospectus minus a percentage spread paid to the investment bank. The spread is a risk transfer premium paid to the investment bank that underwrites the entire value of the offer up front, guaranteeing that the issuing firm will receive the entire proceeds even before the stock makes its opening trade in the market.

The lead underwriter, having paid the issuing company the proceeds, is now free to open trading for the stock at any price deemed acceptable to the buyers in the market, and this is typically *higher* than the "official" offer price. The first level of buyers is composed exclusively of other investment banks making up the selling syndicate that was organized by the lead underwriter to widely disseminate the stock. This first round of buyers purchases the stock around the offer price, keeps some for their own accounts, and then quickly turns around and makes a market for the stock by selling the rest through their nationwide network of offices to second-level buyers at the early rounds of trading at a higher price. This second level of buyers are generally their best and largest institutional portfolio customers, such as pension plans, bank trusts, and fund managers. They buy the stock at the higher markup above the offer price in the prospectus. These institutional managers also keep some stock for themselves and continue to make a market by selling to the third level of buyers composed of smaller fund managers. Individual investors and the smallest fund managers first see the stock available for purchase in the third level or fourth level of trading activity. Small-cap investors and many mutual funds will be hard-pressed to purchase the stock at either of these first two levels of IPO trading. But remember, the real value in the IPO is probably not just the returns earned in the first two-to-four-days of initial trading. Even if small-cap investors buy the stock after this time, the firm's long-term prospects for growth should endure well beyond the introductory market period.

Does Every IPO Stock Earn High Returns?

After watching stock prices in shares of Yahoo! and Amazon.com jump 600 percent in the first year (1997–1998) after their respective IPOs,[8] investors can be lured into high expectations for newly issued shares. Recently (June 1998), shares of the technology IPOs for Software.com, NetGravity, and Inktomi were up 85 percent, 167 percent, and 270 percent, respectively, all within the first *month* of trading.[9] But not every IPO will increase in value sixfold during the first year. Investors in Netscape enjoyed the stock's increase in price to $87 from its 1995 IPO at $28, but then had to endure a three-year drop to around $15 in early 1998.[10] Xylan Corporation, a maker of corporate network switching devices, went public in 1996 with an official offering price of $26 per share, but opened initial trading at $55, and closed above $75. But now, more than two years later, it struggles to trade in the low 20s, while Cisco Systems, the megaleader in the switching industry, continues to acquire many similar small-cap competitors.[11]

Small-cap investors generally anticipate that the majority of emerging IPO firms will grow in value over time, but the questions of which ones will grow the most and by how much are not easily answered. Evidence suggests that underwriters deliberately underprice IPOs compared to the eventual true market equilibrium price in order to provide a profit incentive to the selling syndicate for disseminating the stock among a wide public market.[12] During the initial rounds of trading on the first two-to-three days of the offer, prices on IPOs tend to rise quickly to their eventual equilibrium price creating very significant positive returns. But that rapid short-term gain should not be the focus of the small-cap investor. Instead, buying the stock at the third or fourth level should be done with an eye toward the long-term growth prospects of the small-cap firm. For example, an IPO priced at $12 for three million shares would, after perhaps a 7.5 percent underwriter spread, yield the issuing company $11.10 per share or $33.3 million in proceeds from the lead investment bank. The underwriter might decide to open trading at $12 and shares could be at $13 1/8 at the close of the first day, and then perhaps $14 1/4 after two days of trading. This produces a nice 10 to 17 percent return over the first two days, but the small-cap investor is focused on industry and company growth potential for the next five-to-seven years, when the stock is expected to trade in the mid-40s. The objective of investing in emerging IPOs is to get in on a ground-floor opportunity and realize a strong and consistent growth of value over the long term.

Is Short-Term Profit Taking Okay?

This question is a direct result of how small-cap investors approach the issue of "ultimate value," namely, that point when the stock has reached the expected growth level originally anticipated when the initial trade was executed. There will always be a natural tendency among small-cap investors to want to sell shares in companies that have experienced a significant short-term increase in price. The temptation to "lock in" a certain profit exists whenever recent good news drives stock prices higher, but it is generally a flawed investment strategy. Granted, when a small-cap generates a huge increase in value in the short term, investors want to sell to avoid losing their unrealized "paper gains," which could easily disappear in the ensuing short-term trading horizon. No investor wants to deal with the hindsight regrets of having missed an opportunity to show a profit on portfolio holdings. But the small-cap "entrepreneurial perspective" is not about taking advantage of short-term price volatility. Instead, it is built on a patient tolerance for near-term fluctuations in value, a belief that the business has a potential for truly significant growth as the industry expands and the product market matures, and a long-term vision of where the company can be at its fullest potential.

Going into any small-cap purchase, investors must establish a clear objective for growth, and a definition of what constitutes ultimate value. For example, if an emerging small-cap stock, with 2 percent market share and 35 cents in earnings per share, is purchased at $15 within 45 days of its IPO, the vision might be that this company will ultimately own more than one quarter of the industry's market share, have earnings of more than $4.25 per share, and trade at around $50. If in the first six months the stock is bid up to $28, the small-cap investor is faced with a major decision: Take the nearly 100 percent gain in value now or continue to hold the stock for the longer-term potential.

The following portfolio rule might be helpful in sorting out this dilemma. Any given stock holding represents a certain percentage of the portfolio's overall value. The dollars available from a near-term gain will provide a second round of equity funds that will need to be reinvested. If this total dollar value can be rolled over into a greater number of shares in another small-cap stock with a similar risk-return and industry profile for growth potential, then the sale makes sense. The portfolio will expand the number of shares held, and maintain the targeted ultimate valuation perspective, while growing in terms of assets under management. But if the sale of the stock will simply provide cash that cannot be invested right away (because of no eligible stocks), or that can be invested only into a very similar number of shares (at a higher price per share), then the sale may not produce a measurable position advantage for the portfolio over the long term.

Can Technical Analysis Be Used with Fundamental Analysis?

The answer is a definitive no. It is impossible for small-cap investors to blend the two perspectives into a combined portfolio rationale. Although a significant majority of America's individual investors and many retail stockbrokers claim to use both technical and fundamental analysis, they are, by definition, completely opposite positions in terms of how they view the stock valuation process. Remember from Chapter 4, technical analysis believes the market is inefficient and that past price performance is a valid indicator of future stock values because prices move in nonrandom fashion. Fundamental analysis believes the market is at least weak-form efficient, so prices reflect some degree of the available information and expectations about the economy, the industry, and the firm. The basic reason they cannot be used together is because the use of one nullifies the other. For example, a technical analyst relies on charts that show the small-cap stock's recent price movements and prior volume. This will supposedly isolate consistent "indicators" that will point to time periods when the stock is ready for either upward or downward price changes. There is no macroeconomic, industry, or firm-specific information used in arriving at the stock's expected valuation. So the technical analyst makes stock valuations irrespective of the company's products, markets, management, industry competition and trends, and the health of the overall economy. On the other hand, fundamental analysis views the stock value based on the company's ability to generate future cash flow. The overall economy, the industry, and the firm's management and operations are altogether incorporated into expectations about the company's future earnings which determine the stock's current value. It is entirely a contradiction for a stock's price to be determined by charts of previous price fluctuations as well as by current information about the company's fundamentals. The reality is that true technical analysts do not even care to know what the firm does, in what industry it competes, or how the current competitive market is structured. The only thing they look at is so-called links between prior prices, volume, P/E ratios, and other quantitative measures. This is mutually exclusive from the nature of basic fundamental analysis.

Is There a "Best" Way to Diversify?

Diversification is a direct reflection of the portfolio manager's personal investment philosophy and risk tolerance. Obviously the best way to diversify cannot be known until hindsight reviews the performance after a certain holding period. Small-cap investors cannot establish a truly "optimum" portfolio diversification strategy because there are too many unknown factors associated with the pool of available small-cap stocks. Some firms may appear to provide a level of industry or technology diversification within the small-cap investment strategy, but rapid change and innovation can quickly restructure an emerging industry and the firms in it. A stock that was once considered an Internet access provider might eventually be known as a telecommunications firm. A digital wireless server might, through acquisitions, become a custom satellite manufacturer. And a medical precision instruments firm could turn out to be a testing laboratory supporting several emerging pharmaceutical ventures. Something that was considered "hot" in 1997 might be passé by the end of 1998. Also, a small-cap might very quickly become a mid-cap or large-cap as buying patterns are influenced by new developments in the industry. Transitions in product and service offerings can literally remake an entire industry in a matter of just a few years.

Whether the small-cap investor utilizes an intragroup, intergroup, or international strategy, diversification must focus on stocks that are fundamentally uncorrelated with each other. Even diversifying across several different small-cap mutual funds can create significant changes in portfolio risk over time because of the frequency and accuracy of the rebalancing that takes place in each fund. Some small-cap funds already incorporate provision for holding some mid-cap and large-cap stocks, or long and short positions in stock index futures. These schedules of investments may not be the best fit with a particular small-cap portfolio strategy. The best way to accomplish this is to blend technologies and industries and firm size to bring the expected risk of the overall portfolio in line with the return expectations of the small-cap investment strategy.

Are Stocks Better Than Mutual Funds?

Many small-cap mutual funds provide an excellent means of investing in a wide range of emerging stocks and offer a supposed added benefit of "professional" management. But there are two primary issues to consider when comparing a small-cap stock portfolio to a small-cap mutual fund. First, the reality is that not all professionally managed small-cap mutual funds have similar performance over the same periods of time. And second, the management fees and other related costs can be quite expensive, depending on the fund. Regarding performance, Morningstar and Lipper Analytical Services each provide rankings of mutual fund returns with respect to the risk of the holdings and in comparison to several major indexes. Historically, small-cap funds have very different internal variances in their respective returns. This means that some funds have less price volatility and are therefore a lower risk to the investor than others. Also, small-cap mutual funds typically have a wide range of different returns when compared directly with other funds. So even the decision to invest in small-cap mutual funds does not remove the investor from the risks of internal price fluctuations and dissimilar annual returns. But in the same manner, that does not mean that a private portfolio of individual small-cap stocks will necessarily outperform a competing mutual fund. The former could be structured with a much greater internal variance and be heavily weighted in stocks that are not completely unique from one another.

With respect to costs, many private small-cap portfolios can operate with significantly lower management costs over the long term. Although transaction costs on buying and selling are likely to be higher on a per-trade basis, a less active management style can generally reduce the number of transactions per year and lower the aggregate portfolio administrative expenses. Some public mutual funds may also charge front-end or redemption loads in addition to the quarterly management fees. It is important that small-cap investors establish clearly defined trading policies that simulate the anticipated buying and selling volume in a given year, when comparing a professionally managed fund to the holdings of a private small-cap portfolio. The ultimate trade-off will always focus on whether the risk-adjusted performance of the professionally managed small-cap mutual fund is superior to the private portfolio by an amount greater than any additional costs and management fees. Or, does the private small-cap portfolio have a higher risk-adjusted return after factoring in any cost differentials compared to a public mutual fund.

How Often Are Allocations Rebalanced?

The decision to rebalance a portfolio should not be entered into on a whim based upon some recent short-term volatility in the market. It is a strategic and long-term policy decision based upon the risk-return profile of the small-cap portfolio and the significant change (whether positive or negative) in the realistic prospects of a given firm. Rebalancing the portfolio is not aimed at jumping into a quick upturn on a stock or selling something off only to get in again once a short-term correction has run its course. Remember the portfolio was configured to a certain risk-return and diversification rationale to be positioned for long-term growth in value. Reallocating the funds among the different categories of holdings needs to be a thoughtful and calculated adjustment based upon new information deemed to be critical to the fund's performance over the long term. Typically, a small-cap fund could be rebalanced once every six-to-nine months, and this obviously depends on the contemporary market as well as changes in any unique industry and firm-specific information. Some holdings might remain in their original configuration for one or two years. Others might need more frequent updates in response to the overwhelming level of economic, industry, and firm changes taking place. For the most part, small-cap investors should never implement a reallocation without first thinking through the impact it will have on existing holdings and the long-term performance and risk position of the portfolio.

What Is the Expected Holding Period?

The typical holding period for a small-cap portfolio should be at least five years. Whether the stocks are aimed at emerging growth firms or value companies on the rebound across several fundamentals, the overall objective of the small-cap strategy is not to turn a quick profit. Small-cap firms are making inroads into new and established markets. They are introducing breakthrough technologies with innovative product and service applications. It takes a good deal of time for their financial structures to change dramatically as they experience increased sales, cost efficiencies of scale from larger production output, better profitability, and improvements in the balance sheet. Senior management talent will also be expanded and improved as the company matures and widens its industry focus. Small-cap investors should be ready to participate in the firm's prospects for the long haul. The small-cap portfolio should never be viewed as a short-term investment tactic aimed at cornering a quick upturn in an industry or one company's newfound fame. Volatility in the short-term cannot be differentiated as negative or positive before the fact. Buying and selling patterns can be very fickle as new information streams into the investment community. Small-cap investing is all about screening for strong potential among industries and specific companies and then putting money into those places with the best prospects for growth. There are many stories on Wall Street about either waiting too long to get in on a new industry or selling out far too early on a firm that continued to experience phenomenal growth long after it had a minor, and short-term, downturn.

Notes

1. See Reinganum, Marc, 1983. "Portfolio Strategies Based on Market Capitalization," *Journal of Portfolio Management*, Winter, pp. 29–36. Reinganum, 1992. "A revival of the Small-Firm Effect," *Journal of Portfolio Management*, Spring, pp. 55–62. Jacobs and Levy, 1989. "Forecasting the Size Effect," *Financial Analysts Journal*, May–June, pp. 38–54; "Beta Beaten," *Economist*, March 7, p. 87.

2. Berk, Jonathan, 1997. "Does Size Really Matter?" *Financial Analysts Journal*, Sept–Oct, 12–18.

3. Rogalski and Tinic, 1986. "The January Size Effect: Anomaly or Risk Measurement?" *Financial Analysts Journal*, Nov–Dec, pp. 63–70.

4. Jensen, Johnson, and Mercer, 1997. "New Evidence on Size and Price-to-Book Effects in Stock Returns," *Financial Analysts Journal*, Nov–Dec, pp. 34–42.

5. See such periodicals as *The IPO Reporter* (2 World Trade Center, #18, New York, NY 10048); *The IPO Monitor* at www.ipomonitor.com.

6. See such sources as *Bull and Bear Financial Newspaper* (PO Box 4267, Winter Park, FL 32793); *The Investment Reporter* at http://ipo-tip.com; *OTC Research's Financial Network* at 1040 Great Plain Avenue, Needham, MA 02192.

7. Greenwald, John, 1998. "Crazy Stock Ride," *Time*, July 20, pp. 42–43.

8. Vrana, Debora, 1998. "Summer Swoon Lingers but IPO Biz May Heat Up," *Los Angeles Times*, Section D, July 13, pp. 1, 6.

9. See Greenwald, 1998.

10. Rynecki, David, 1998. "Hype Hot for Broadcast.com Despite Red Flags," *USA Today*, Section C, July 14, p. 1.

11. Hua, Vanessa, 1998. "Nimble Xylan Dances on Giants' Turf," *Los Angeles Times,* August 25, p. D2.

12. See such works as Logue, Dennis, 1973. "On the Pricing of Unseasoned Equity Issues: 1965–69, *Journal of Financial and Quantitative Analysis*, January, pp. 91–103. Ibottson, Roger, 1975. "Price Performance of Common Stock Issues," *Journal of Finance*, September, pp. 1027–1042. Rock, Kevin, 1986. "Why New Issues Are Underpriced," *Journal of Financial Economics*, Jan–Feb, pp. 187–212. Miller and Reilly, 1987. "Mispricing, Uncertainty, and Return in Initial Public Offerings," *Financial Management*, Summer, pp. 33–38. Newton, David, 1990. "Underwriting Spreads as an Indicator of the Degree of Mispricing in Unseasoned Equity Offerings," *Dissertation Abstracts International*. Newton, David, 1993. "How Underwriting Spreads Are Assigned to IPOs," *SBIDA Proceedings,* February, pp. 138–147.

Performance Expectations and Conclusion

Careful Consideration

Becoming a successful small-cap investor requires vision and tremendous patience during the volatile movements that characterize the short-term market. These are required in professional fund management, retail brokerage, and individual investing alike. The small-cap portfolio strategy will obviously require a good deal of research, analysis, entrepreneurial perspective, close monitoring, and perseverance through periods of strong performance as well as periodic downturns. In early August 1998, the morning newspaper's business section reported that "U.S. stock funds continue to trail their European counterparts," with domestic American stock funds up an average of 9.7 percent, while German, French, and British funds are up an average of 31.1 percent.[1] It could be very easy for the small-cap investor to reason that the stock market has suddenly changed its focus, or that American firms are now poised for a long-term lag behind foreign companies. That same front-page story also presented the "top-ten" funds for the last 4 weeks, 12 months, and 5 years. The two most recent periods (4 weeks and 12 months) were led by none other than a small-cap fund (up 65.5 percent for 4 weeks and 93.2 percent for 12 months), which also ranked third for the last five years, up 294 percent. In fact, all three listings included some small-cap funds. So even though the European funds seemed to be making larger gains thus far in 1998, the one-month, one-year, and five-year periods have strong representation from the small-cap market segment.

Investors must recognize that recent activity in any stock market period cannot be interpreted as the new trend or an all-inclusive commentary on performance expectations for a well-positioned small-cap portfolio. August 4, 1998 will no doubt be logged as a significant milestone in the history of the U.S. stock market, as the Dow Jones Industrial Average plummeted 299 points with volume of nearly 950 million shares, on news of worsening U.S. trade with Southeast Asia.[2] A closer look at the facts and figures of the day shows that many small-cap firms trading on the NASDAQ were up significantly, and 18 firms closed at their all-time high price.

The Pool to Watch

The pool of small-cap stocks is composed of some 6300 individual companies. And yet the aggregate market capitalization of all these firms is only equal to the combined market value of just General Electric and Microsoft.[3] There is less information readily available for the vast majority of these small-cap companies when compared to large firms, and there are considerably fewer professional securities analysts following these stocks. In fact, while 98 percent of small-caps listed on the Russell 2000 Index have at least one analyst covering them, there remains only an average of about five securities analysts regularly tracking each company. This means that of those analysts watching the stock, there may be only two or three third-party (objective) annual earnings commentaries prepared each year. Comprehensive information about small-cap firms will not be found among the pages of the Moody's Industrial Manual or the Standard and Poor's Stock Guide. Now consider that three out of every five micro-cap stocks do not even have a single analyst following them on any kind of a regular basis. This lack of consistent tracking and reliable information about company earnings and operations remains a paradox, because the public market for trading small-caps is both wide open with incredible opportunity and at the same time fraught with significant risks.

Larger-Cap Comparisons

The decision to invest in small-cap stocks will always be challenged as to its relative merits. Comparisons will no doubt be made to the mid-cap and large-cap stocks that "could have been" invested in, or the international stocks that will at some point show a short-term gain while most small-cap prices are down. When the largest companies announce their quarterly earnings in the prominent financial listings in *The Wall Street Journal* and *Barron's,* investors will try to draw conclusions as to what the results mean for smaller firms. Investors understand that comprehensive earnings per-share reports for small-cap companies ASM, CFM, and MIM will not be found among the much-anticipated data for 3M, IBM, and GM. Typically, the small-caps do not have any measurable influence on the Dow Jones Industrial Average, but the movement of the broad underlying markets will cause small-cap investors to ponder their portfolios in light of the financial results that larger companies are experiencing.

Front-page stories generally make only minor summary comments about the activity of the Russell 2000 Index. For example, a recent regional daily newspaper's business section headlines featured the two words "small companies," but the overall article content was primarily focused elsewhere, dealing with the broader market's attempted rebound from several weeks of downturns. It stated that "some of the worst hit sectors [referring to small-caps] helped lead the market higher, as smaller companies' stocks, which had plunged almost 14 percent to a 1998 low in the last three weeks, rebounded with the Russell 2000 Index rising 7.93 points, or 2.31 percent."[4] But in the very next sentence, the report moved into coverage of large-cap NASDAQ technology stocks and the likelihood that larger firms remained overpriced as their earnings are expected to be lower because of on-going concerns about Asian consumer markets. No specific small-cap stocks were discussed, and the article never made it back to the small company headline, as it closed out with a review of various key macroeconomic indicators and the movement of the Dow Jones Industrial Average since the first of the year.

The reality is that mainstream financial news media do not provide even minor attention to small-cap or micro-cap companies, let alone comprehensive coverage of key firms in this sector and specific earnings reports or product development information. A recent perusal of four prominent daily business periodicals turned up only minor coverage of small-cap stocks. These were primarily casual referrals to the Russell 2000 Index in the context of a headline report dealing with overall market activity or a large company's earnings and recent return performance. By chance, one newspaper presented a few mutual fund highlights from Lipper Analytical Services that compared 15 categorical indexes such as "emerging markets," "European region," "growth and income," and "utilities." The small-cap index was at the bottom of the list as the worst performer over the last four weeks (off 12.4 percent). But just below that listing, a sidebar noted IBC's

Money Fund Report performance summary for about a dozen international small-cap funds. All but two had a positive return over the last four weeks, and 10 of the 12 funds had 1998 returns in excess of 20 percent (the high was up 40.5 percent and the average was up 28.2 percent).[5]

Correlations with Other Investments

There have been numerous studies published over the last 70 years that try to codify exact performance relationships between various domestic common stock, international common stock, bond, money market, and mutual fund investments. The last 20 years has produced a gradual increase in the number of studies that compare small-cap stocks to mid-cap and large-cap issues. Within the time frame that this book has been compiled and written, the most recent seven months (January through July 1998) have been considered anything but a good time for small-cap investing. A $10,000 investment in the Russell 2000 Index on January 1, 1998, would have dropped in value to $9900 (a 1 percent decrease). Many financial and securities analysts are quick to make numerous near-term comparisons between small-caps and a wide range of alternative investments. These, however, completely misunderstand the entrepreneurial perspective of small-cap investing. And many times, these shortsighted comparisons are made just as the small-cap market segment is experiencing a slight downturn and other potential investment holdings are riding an upswing. For example, a recent graph in the financial press summarized the 1998 Lipper Analytical Services year-to-date (YTD) average return performance of the 30 largest U.S. blue-chip stock mutual funds, international stock funds, and small-cap funds. It also had the total YTD returns for money market accounts from the IBC Money Fund Report, the Merrill Lynch average long-term Treasury bond and municipal bonds, and gold bullion. The results showed that international stocks were now leading the pack in 1998, up 19.7 percent through the first eight months. Blue chips were up 11.0 percent, Treasuries earned 6.0 percent, muni-bonds 3.9 percent, money markets 2.8 percent, and gold bullion was up just 0.6 percent. Meanwhile, small-cap stocks were up only 3.7 percent.[6] The report was quick to point out that small-caps were doing poorly, being outperformed by the other two major stock groups, both bond types, and returning just slightly more than a money market account. Pundits of small-cap stocks often draw sweeping conclusions based upon these types of short-term comparisons, challenging the viability of these stocks and even the prior long-term track record of superior performance.

Forget Near-Term Timing

In addition to the numerous shortsighted comparisons made between small-caps and other investment alternatives, there are also many published reports focused on the strategy of trying to time small-cap buy and sell positions. The most interesting issue is that many of these near-term timing ploys are built on the kind of evidence presented in the previous section. Many investment strategists argue that small-caps, like other stocks, bonds, gold, and money markets, can be analyzed to find the best "time" to buy in (just before the next short-term price rise), and when to sell out (immediately prior to the upcoming price drop). The thinking goes in one of two common directions. First, there are those who advocate the "formulamatic" approach, that small-cap investors need only follow a few simple steps and then high returns will just happen. This is related to a second mentality that subconsciously ascribes a "guarantee" of high returns to small-cap investing. Each of these lines of reasoning uses a relatively shorter-term investment horizon for expectations, which is very dangerous when approaching the small-cap market segment.

Owning stock in smaller firms is not like the nine-month timing associated with buying a call option or going long on margin in silver futures. In each of these contracts, the investor is not really investing at all, but merely speculating that a particular trend will be realized over the next 30 to 40 weeks. The small-cap investor must recognize that *true* investing means taking a joint stock ownership in a company alongside the founder and senior executives. Exploiting near-term timing and quarterly earnings trends is entirely counter to the entrepreneurial perspective, and the overwhelming majority of empirical studies of such have produced sketchy and highly inconsistent evidence that cannot support it as a portfolio strategy.[7]

Earnings Expectations

Among Wall Street analysts, the core focus for virtually all large-cap and many mid-cap common stock valuations remains the tried-and-true expectations of a company's quarterly earnings, and the subsequent report of the firm's actual profit performance. The most common time frame for this twofold process comes at the end of March, June, September, and December, for those companies with traditional calendar fiscal years. The broader markets eagerly anticipate the release of financial data from companies' quarterly 10-K forms filed with the Securities and Exchange Commission. For example, sometime around late February most securities analysts start to reconcile unaudited January and February sales figures with revenue forecasts for the year that were made back in October, November, and December of the previous year.

Figure 12–1 shows the typical process by which the market values a given stock during the regular earnings cycles of the fiscal year. A close watch of gross margins and overhead expenses allows analysts to target certain levels of *expected* after-tax income and free cash flow based upon reasonable expectations with regard to a firm's typical financial ratios and outstanding debt obligations. Optimistic forecasts spur demand and prices rise. Pessimistic expectations encourage selling and prices drop. Mixed reviews can force many investors to wait for more news before they commit one way or the other. The anticipation of how a particular company "might" perform is still only half the story. As the third month of the quarter winds down, the expectations become more clearly focused and the sentiment can accumulate even stronger activity to buy or sell the stock. The story for the fiscal quarter officially closes out when the actual figures are released and compared to the expectations that have guided trading during the last six-to-eight weeks.

When the dust settles, analysts turn their attention to the first round of new information that comes early on in the subsequent period (in this case, April, May, and June). Second quarter expectations are now compared to the initial reports about revenues, market share, product introductions, costs, pending deals, and such to gauge how closely analysts' forecasts are to tangible company operations. The same scenario from the first quarter is played out as the end of June approaches, and once again actual results will either confirm or contrast the expectations of traders. Stepping back from these two fiscal quarters on the first tier, a second tier of annual forecasts begins to take shape. This will come more and more into focus as the third quarter winds down and the fourth quarter remains the only questionable data for the fiscal year. At the close of the fiscal year, the true annual earnings will again either confirm or contradict analysts' expectations, and the stock will experience buying or selling or waiting based on the accuracy of the forecasts.

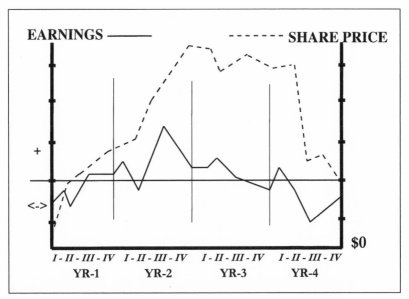

FIGURE 12–1   Relationship of Earnings and Share Price

The final step back is at the third tier and puts each fiscal year within the context of the much broader investment horizon for three, four, or five years worth of analysts' expectations. The reconciliation of earnings expectations with the actual results of firm performance is the basis of fundamental common stock valuation. Trading in small-cap stocks is unique with respect to earnings expectations because there is a much wider discrepancy in the access and reliability of company information when compared to large firms. The reality is that small-cap investors will likely have less information to work with when analyzing stocks for potential portfolio inclusion. But even though the more traditional data sources apparently cater to the larger-cap stocks, small-cap investors who are willing to work hard at research can still obtain a solid basis of pertinent information from which to form investment decisions.

Conclusions and Perspectives

The prospects for outstanding returns from carefully screened small-cap investments remain strong. New companies, new technologies, brand-new industries, and new acquisition deals constantly create new opportunities for investors who can take an entrepreneurial perspective with a vision toward longer-term growth. The challenge comes in locating potential growth while it is still unrealized. Small-cap investors are faced with the task of assembling a pool of companies that fit the best profile within an overall marketing, operations, managerial, and financial context. There is no way to know for sure that a small public company will automatically grow into a highly successful and profitable mid-cap or large-cap firm. The decision to plan and implement a small-cap investment strategy is far more complicated than simply choosing a handful of relatively tiny companies, placing their common stocks in portfolio, and then standing back to wait for their share prices to all increase sixfold over the next two years. No one can guarantee that just because a firm is small and somewhat new to the competitive industry that the only place for the stock price to go will be up. Many smaller companies that are striving to gain a solid foothold within an industry in terms of sales and market share, technology, and distribution networks may never really succeed at all.

Lessons from Venture Capital

The venture capital industry is characterized along the following lines. During the course of a typical fiscal quarter, a venture capital company receives perhaps 500 business plans from various firms. These are processed through as many as five or six tiers of screening in order to yield around a dozen "potential" investments. After several more rounds of review and meetings, maybe two or three of these companies will merit investment. This process resumes the next quarter, and the quarter after that, and over the course of one year the venture capital firm has invested in 10 companies. As with small-cap investing, this strategy is clearly based on fundamental analysis and diversification among different holdings. The mark of a successful venture capitalist is not based on locating 10 companies that will produce high-end performance over the next three years. Instead, investment success comes when five of the firms are actually doing poorly, three are hovering around breakeven, one is showing strong profitability, and another has become a true "star," growing in value by some ninefold. It is finding two good firms among the initial candidates, and repeating this process on a continuous basis that makes the venture capital grow over time. Small-cap investing is very similar to this venture capital process. The screening process should not be expected to produce a 100 percent success ratio. (Refer back to Figure 10–1.) The small-cap portfolio will likely have some losers, some at breakeven, with a few doing well, and one or two stars boasting astronomical growth. The portfolio should continue to screen potential investments, maintain a diversification strategy, and periodically rebalance holdings based on performance. The primary concern will always be the holding period necessary for a company to realize strong growth performance.

Three possible scenarios can either delay or significantly alter the long-awaited success of a promising small-cap stock. These may even happen in combination with each other to further compound the company's negative performance over time. The following sections provide some concluding thoughts to consider about how some of the best and brightest stars among the small-cap potential opportunities can fall short of their investment performance targets because the company either (a) loses track of the true industry direction, (b) loses its technological position to better, faster, and more efficient design innovations, or (c) loses production cost efficiencies to larger firms with significant economies of scale.

Loss of Industry Direction

Many small-cap firms chart a course for a certain objective, fully believing that the industry is headed in a certain direction. They can easily pour tens of millions of dollars into what is believed to be the correct strategy for the expected competitive environment, only to see the market evolve and develop in a completely different direction. Companies may commit personnel and facilities to a sales campaign that ultimately falls short of buyers' expectations. Small-cap investors can easily be lured into a false sense of security because a firm seems to be at the forefront of an emerging industry, makes exciting claims about its products, and generates some promising sales early on in what is essentially an untested market. For example, in August of 1996, J. Brian O'Neill founded TeleSpectrum, Incorporated, by combining six small telemarketing companies into a single business entity with 7800 employees in seven states. Small-cap investors were very optimistic that the firm would see rapid sales growth for years to come as new clients were developed and added to its aggregate base of business. But in just its second year of operations (1997), almost $15 million of its overall $43 million in sales (more than 30 percent) came from one account, MBNA. The rapid sales growth from 1996 to 1997 was almost entirely due to adding this one large account to the original base of about $25 million in combined sales among the original six telemarketing firms. The stock peaked at around $21 per share. Then MBNA moved all their telemarketing operations in-house and TeleSpectrum lost a full one-third of its revenues. Today the firm employs less than 5000 workers, has closed more than half of its 25 call centers, and the stock price has dropped about 86.5 percent to around $3 per share.[8] This small company believed that the industry was moving in the direction where large firms would subcontract out their telemarketing operations to specialty firms. But recent trends seem to show that many larger companies now believe it is most cost-effective and productive to manage this function internally. TeleSpectrum's strategy was aimed at rapid growth through the consolidated business of dozens of small firms. Now it appears that these smaller business units would be more profitable individually serving a few small clients, rather than joined under a parent company umbrella targeting large-scale telemarketing functions for big firms. Small-cap investors must be careful to sort real potential from wishful thinking.

Loss of Technological Position

It is not uncommon for firms with a supposed "innovative edge" at one point in their development to find themselves in the awkward position of trying to sell an outdated product or service just a year or two later. Technology can advance so rapidly in some industries that firms must be able to allocate significant budgets to ongoing research and development just to try and keep pace with the leaders in the market, as well as the next wave of new companies breaking into the industry with their own innovations. The ability to hold onto the leadership position in an emerging market will likely require several rounds of additional capital investment. A great product or service concept today might be very outdated in no time. Think about how dramatic it was to see someone talking on a "mobile phone" in 1985. The handset was the size of a World War II field walkie-talkie, with a 12-inch telescoping antenna and a two-foot coiled wire connected to a 7-pound battery power pack that looked like a lunch box. Back then, Tandy Corporation was one of the leaders in the mobile phone industry and sold three basic models through hundreds of Radio Shack stores around the country. Typical units sold for between $750 to $1000 and service charges were in the range of $3 per minute. However, in less than six years the company was no longer a viable competitor as innovative cellular technology and microcircuitry reduced phones to the size of a person's palm. Today cell phones sell for around $49 to $89, and service plans are priced in the range of 30 cents per minute. Numerous small-cap firms looked great when mobile communications emerged as a promising new technology, but now the industry has moved far beyond simple antenna-based mobile communications into what is now termed *digital satellite data relay*. Once again, small-cap investors need to decide which firms are staying on the forefront of technology and which are just in the market for the short term.

Loss of Production Efficiency

There are also numerous cases where a small-cap firm appears to be right on the cutting edge of what should become a widely used new manufacturing innovation, or operations procedure, and yet the company never fully realizes its potential and the small-cap investors are left to ponder forever "what could have been." This is often the case when larger, more established firms in the same or similar industry enter the manufacturing race with significantly lower costs of production. Because of economies of scale, large companies can have better logistics, greater output capacity, and lower overhead, labor, and materials on a per-unit basis than the smaller-scale business. A small Malvern, Pennsylvania, tool company, Ultrafast, Incorporated, has recently developed a viable handheld computer-controlled ratchet assembly tool that measures the perfect tightness for bolts used in hundreds of commercial applications, including the automobile and aerospace industries. The technology uses a transducer to measure ultrasonic waves sent through generic manufacturing bolts to measure the precise tightening based on the travel time of the wave through the bolt. By lowering the chance that a bolt will fail, it reduces the number of bolts needed and saves manufacturing time and money. The firm had revenues of about $10 million and 32 employees in 1998, and it expects to grow to more than $200 million in revenue, with over 500 employees by 2002.[9] The key issue in this case is that the company *expects* to grow sales 20-fold in four years. Whether that will actually transpire is subject to several factors. The company may in fact be poised to capture a large initial stake in the huge market for bolt assembly tools. But other well-established and significantly larger tool manufacturers may already be better positioned to dominate this industry because of an existing strong presence among commercial accounts and substantially lower unit costs of production.

Closing Remarks

Just because a firm has a small market capitalization does not guarantee it will be a great investment. But just because a company is a small-cap does not mean it will never take a leadership position in its industry and, in the process, reward early investors for their vision and patience. Categorically, small-cap stocks merit serious and thoughtful consideration from investors. Many smaller firms will in time grow to become large and highly profitable. A consistent and systematic approach to screening small-cap stocks based on economic, industry, and firm-specific information forms the basis for a long-term small-cap investment strategy. Diversification combined with periodic reviews of the portfolio's asset allocation should position the small-cap investor for extraordinary growth over the long term. Although past performance is in no way an exact indicator of future performance, the small-cap investor should expect that an entrepreneurial perspective will probably be able to take advantage of the growth potential among companies involved in ongoing innovation and rapidly evolving emerging industries. Short-term volatility will require patience, and not every stock selected will turn out to be the next Microsoft. But entrepreneurial ingenuity will very likely continue throughout the next century to develop new products and services for new buyers and markets, and investors with an eye toward that future will look back one day and be glad they bought into certain companies when they did.

One Last Update

As this book nears its release date, small-caps have experienced several significant positive gains since the fall of 1998. During the spring of 1998, the stock market dropped amid poor earnings reports and lingering fears about Asian economics. Since last summer, the mega-caps of the Dow Jones Industrial Average have added 2,750 points (+34.6%) to 10,700 while the large-cap dominant S&P 500 Index is up 310 points (+29.5%) to around 1,350. But the hot growth, emerging technologies, that define the smaller-caps have performed much better. The NASDAQ Composite has gained 1,120 points (+81.1%), fueled by numerous Internet, computer networking, biotech, precision instrument, electronics, hardware/software fast-growth, and entrepreneurial firms. Further, the Russell 2000 Small-Cap Index has added 130 points, from the 300 level to just over 430, a gain of +43.3%.

The Dallas-based fall '98 IPO Broadcast.com ran up to more than $130 per share and is now being acquired by Yahoo! for $5.7 billion. Many small-cap investors are being rewarded quite nicely for their interest in this small-cap that introduced live-event broadcasting to the Web. Dozens of other small-caps stocks have demonstrated excellent earnings and great price appreciation, and yet the debate still rages as to the viability of this sector for modern portfolio strategies. Paul Lim recently wrote for *The LA Times* that it's time to get small-cap companies out of the normal asset allocation mix for stock portfolios. He sites the last five years (1994–1999) during which the S&P 500 has "generated a total return of +220.5%, (while) in that same period, the Russell 2000 Index gained just 58.4%."[10] Mr. Lim notes that during the 1991–1993 period just before that, the small-caps had substantially higher returns than the S&P 500, but questions the underlying rationale for including small-caps in portfolios.

This type of commentary disregards the solid and consistent track-record of higher returns over the long term that has accrued to investors with the entrepreneurial perspective for buying (and staying with) small-cap stocks. Many other recently released reports are now claiming that if Internet-related firms are removed from the Russell 2000 and NASDAQ gains, small-cap stocks don't look very appealing at all.[11] However, these researchers fail to realize that these growing Internet companies were all small-caps at some point during the last six years, and their potential price appreciation is a function of their entrepreneurial spirit to pioneer new technologies, products, and services to several emerging industries within this technology sector. And many "no-name" small-caps today, will be well-known big winners five years from now. To pull them out of these indexes and then ridicule small-caps is the same as removing IBM, Microsoft, and Disney from the DJIA and stating that big companies don't perform very well.

A widely circulated full-page advertisement for The New York Stock Exchange captures what is truly the essence of small-cap investing. The picture shows around four dozen nondescript and differently colored middle class homes sitting side by side, row by row on streets with porches, telephone poles, wires, and trees. The caption reads as follows:

> In whose garage will America's next success story be written? It could be anyone's. We live in a country where someone can start out with no more than an idea, and spawn a global industry that changes the way we all live....we celebrate that spirit...because equity is all about the future.

Small-cap investing is forward-thinking, full of potential, necessarily expectant, and open to a wide range of possible outcomes. Small-cap investing represents the very best of what makes the capital markets exciting and dynamic over the long-term. Small-cap investing is all about profiting on the future . . . and the future is taking shape right now!

Notes

1. Block, Sandra, 1998. "European Funds Continue to Lead the Way," *USA Today*, August 3, p. 3B.

2. Jacobsen, Sally, 1998. "Leading Economic Indicators Off a Notch," *The Philadelphia Inquirer*, August 5, pp. C1, C3.

3. Lim, Paul J., 1998. "It Will Pay You to Do Your Homework," *Los Angeles Times,* July 28, p. D6.

4. Fuerbringer, Jonathan, 1998. "Stocks of Small Companies Revive, Pulling Broader Markets Higher," *New York Times*, August 7, pp. D1, D5.

5. 1998, "Mutual Fund Spotlight," *USA Today*, August 6, p. 6B.

6. "Investment Derby," *Los Angeles Times,* July 26, 1998, p. D2.

7. See summary sections of "Tests of Semi-Strong Form Efficiency" in Smith, Proffitt, and Stephens, 1992. *Investments* (St. Paul, MN: West Publishing), Chapters 4, 8, and 12. See also Dorfman, J., 1989. "Investors Can Get Help with Earnings Surprises," *Wall Street Journal*, August 7, p. C1. Roll, R., 1980. "Performance Evaluation and Benchmark Errors," *Journal of Portfolio Management*, Summer, pp. 5–12. Lorie, Dodd, and Kimpton, 1985. *The Stock Market: Theories and Evidences* (Homewoord, IL: Irwin), Chapter 11.

8. Binzen, Peter, 1998. "On Business," *The Philadelphia Inquirer*, August 3, pp. C1, C5.

9. Mount, Ian, 1998. "Giving Bolts a New Twist," *The Philadelphia Inquirer*, August 3, pp. C1, C3.

10. Lim, Paul J., 1999. "Questioning Small-Caps' Status as a Core Buy," *The Los Angeles Times*, April 4, S1.

11. For example: Guerrieri, C.A., 1999. "The '.com' Effect on Small-Cap Growth," *Consulting Group Research Bulletin*, April 19, Vol. 2, No. 11, pp. 1–7.

INDEX

Index note to the reader: illustrations are indicated by the numbers in bold print.

ABOUT THE AUTHOR

David Newton is Associate Professor of Entrepreneurial Finance at
California's Westmont College. Dr. Newton has written or contributed to
nearly 50 articles in entrepreneurship and finance publications, including
Business Week, Money, Entrepreneur, and *Success*, and is the author of
Entrepreneurial Ethics, a book described by *INC* magazine as "…a land-
mark work."